WASHINGTON ROCK

A CLIMBER'S GUIDE TO

WASHINGTON ROCK

DARRINGTON
INDEX
LEAVENWORTH

DON BROOKS

illustrated by
DAVID WHITELAW

THE MOUNTAINEERS • SEATTLE

THE MOUNTAINEERS: Organized in 1906
"...to explore, study, preserve, and enjoy
the natural beauty of the Northwest."

Published by The Mountaineers
306 - 2nd Ave. W., Seattle, Washington 98119

Published simultaneously in Canada by
Douglas & McIntyre, Ltd.
1615 Venables Street
Vancouver, British Columbia V5L 2H1

Printed in the United States of America

Book design by David Whitelaw

Library of Congress Cataloging in Publication Data

Brooks, Don.
    A climber's guide to Washington rock.

    Includes index.
    1. Rock climbing — Washington (State) — Darrington
— Guide-books.   2. Rock climbing — Washington (State)
— Index — Guide-books.   3. Rock climbing — Washington
(State) — Leavenworth — Guide-books.   4. Darrington
(Wash.) — Description and travel — Guide-books.
5. Index (Wash.) — Description and travel — Guide-
books.   6. Leavenworth (Wash.) — Description and
travel — Guide-books.   I. Title.   II. Title: Wash-
ington rock.
GV199.42.W22D373   1981   917.97   81-18742
ISBN 0-89886-046-6   AACR2

09876
5432

Thanks are due to the many people who offered suggestions, information and encouragement, but a few people must be singled out for special mention. Most important are Chris Syrjala, my wife, who is so patient and understanding with almost everything I do, and David Whitelaw, who came into the project and provided such magnificent illustrations. A very special thanks to the many people who have taught, endured and climbed with me for the last 13 years. May we all have many more together.

Don Brooks

Working with Don on this project and making all the drawings and topos for this book was a bit like going back through time. Many faces came smiling through the years, but I'd especially like to thank Duane Constantino, John Downing, Chris Greyell, Reilly Moss, and John Studebaker for their optimism, patience, and friendship through it all.

David Whitelaw

CONTENTS

PREFACE

Washington Rock is the fourth guide covering the state's major crags in the Darrington, Index and Leavenworth areas. The first, published in 1965 by Fred Beckey and Eric Bjornstad, listed approximately 100 routes and was limited to the Leavenworth area. Ten years later, the second, by Rich Carlstad and Don Brooks, was released. This guide covered Index as well as Leavenworth and contained over 200 routes, including some 45 new Leavenworth routes as well as dozens of free ascents of old aid routes. In 1976, Fred Beckey issued another guide containing route information for Darrington and Index. This fourth guide, *Washington Rock,* is now needed, mostly due to the new route explosion in all three areas which pushes this volume to over 300 routes.

Washington Rock reflects the changes evident in the Washington rock-climbing scene today. The previous guides gave minimal information about individual climbs in order to train climbers in route finding, thus making them more competent to travel safely in the mountains. This guide gives more detail, allowing people to push their limits more fully. People who disagree with this format are invited to disregard topo pages or to move afield to discover new crags — Washington has many.

Other areas potentially falling into the scope of *Washington Rock* are Beacon Rock, the Skagit and Whatcom County areas and the high-country spots. Because these areas are covered in other guides, they are not included here. Those interested may refer to *Oregon Rock* by

Jeff Thomas (in press in 1982) and *Boulders and Cliffs: Climber's Guide to Lowland Rock in Skagit and Whatcom Counties* by Dallas M. Kloke. Beyond these areas, other small cliffs, tucked away in secret places, exist and someday may be publicized.

As always in a work of this scope, minor errors will remain. Corrections, additions and new route information are requested in order to make future volumes more accurate and effective. Please send comments and information to Don Brooks, c/o The Mountaineers • Books, 306 2nd Ave. West, Seattle, Washington 98119.

Safety Considerations

Most of the users of this book will not need to be reminded that, since terrain changes rapidly, weather changes even faster, and safety always depends on the preparation, skill, and judgment of the climbers involved, the descriptions in this book are not representations that the routes described are "safe" and do not list every possible hazard that the climber may confront. A large part of the excitement and challenge of hiking and climbing is meeting risks that can't be predicted and are not present at home. It is one of climbing's basic axioms that when you climb, you assume these risks, and must assume responsibility for your own safety. Any guidebook, no matter how comprehensive, can only give you limited advice and information.

The publisher

INTRODUCTION

Washington is well known throughout the climbing world for its remaining volcanoes and its horrible mountain weather. The hundreds of peaks scattered throughout the state are less well known but are beginning to draw more attention. Usually overlooked are several outstanding rock-climbing areas tucked into the foothills on either side of the Cascades.

Leavenworth, the state's classic area, lies on the comparatively dry east side of the mountains. Indeed, local boosters claim 300 days of sunshine each year. Just what constitutes "a day of sunshine," however, is up for grabs! While ice and snow climbs are found scattered around the area in the winter months, in mild years it's possible to find rock climbs in the Peshastin area in any month. Generally though, from April to October one stands a much better chance of good conditions than in the winter months.

Besides Leavenworth's good weather, its superb rock and its variety of problems are unequaled in the Northwest. Here, climbers of all abilities can find beautiful lines to dream of and to climb. Midway, a 5.5 route, is a perfect example. Few climbs of this difficulty combine such individually delightful moves with such a classic line. Virtually all the routes on Midnight, on the other end of the rating scale, tell much the same story.

Leavenworth is also an area for learning. Faces and cracks of all difficulties are found on small crags in Icicle Canyon as well as on all the major cliffs. Slab and face climbs are also found in the unique Peshastin Pinnacles. In the early days at Leavenworth, the cliffs were considered "practice areas." Today's climbers still practice here in preparation for moving into the mountains of the world, but hundreds and perhaps thousands have found Leavenworth to be an end in itself.

Index, on the west side of Stevens Pass, is quite different. Major differences include the poorer weather, the proximity of the few cliffs and the intimidating nature of all but a few of the routes.

While rain is a constant threat at Index, the winter can vary from T-shirt to waterfall-climbing weather. In summer months it can become torrid on the Upper Wall, but moderate temperatures are the general rule here. Just remember that it's generally a poor idea to leave the cagoule at home when climbing at Index.

The climbs themselves vary from a number of challenging aid routes to many steep, free cracks to a fairly small number of climbs under 5.9. Experienced climbers will find the area exhilarating, while those not so seasoned can find tremendous opportunities for learning aid as well as for working up through the ranks of crack climbs.

Darrington is the state's youngest and least mature area. As such, the few pioneers in the area maintain a tremendous amount of enthusiasm for this still-developing area. Face/slab climbs on solid granite are the rule here, but occasional cracks and aid routes are also found.

The Darrington weather is probably even worse than that of Index, some 25 air miles to the south. Approaches are generally more difficult, route finding can be challenging and protection is difficult. These complications, however, along with the unique face/slab climbing add a tremendous dimension to the state's climbing possibilities.

In the last few years, climbers have seen a number of major changes in these areas besides new routes. Climbing seems to have lost some of its fad appeal. This may be attributed to the high cost of equipment as well as to the transient interests of many people. The people active today tend to be more serious than their counterparts of five years ago; indeed, the "average" climber of today is probably a standard or two better than the "average" climber of a half decade ago. Better equipment and training methods have had their effect as well. More people are also traveling to other areas, passing information and trends around. The rapidly rising standards of the world are reflected in Washington as well—more 5.12 routes are found in this guide than 5.11 routes in the previous one.

Although it will probably never take over here, a measure of standardization has hit the Northwest, much to the sorrow of some. This area has traditionally been the most relaxed of the major climbing centers in that it has lacked much of the peer pressure so evident in California, Colorado and the East. "Mellow" is still a good definition of most Northwest climbers, but a growing number of climbers here are involved in pushing the limits higher than ever before. Virtually all local climbers are alpinists as well as rock climbers, but there is perhaps a greater tendency than previously to emphasize pure rock.

Perhaps the biggest factor in the rise of standards, apart from physical conditioning, is psychological. Many younger climbers don't have to overcome the psychological barrier of 5.10 in quite the same way as their predecessors. Originally defined as the "ultimate," 5.10 is still a mystical number to many veterans. Many of today's 20 year olds correctly see 5.10, 5.11 or 5.12 as numbers on an infinite scale. Limits are placed on individuals by themselves, not by a set of numbers in a rating system.

Many of these concerns, of course, have little or no effect on 95 percent of the people climbing today. They climb for fun or companionship, to be outdoors and for many other reasons. Fortunately, 90 percent of the climbs listed here fall into the "possible" category for 90 percent of these people—if not this year, then maybe next. . . .

HISTORY

Washington, by American standards, has a long, color-ful climbing history, and Northwest mountaineers have left their mark on the world, mainly in the great ranges of Alaska and Asia. Even though local rock-climbing areas are virtually unknown outside Washington, many of the local personalities like Fred Beckey and Jim Madsen are well known to climbers around the country. This section will look generally at some of these personalities and lay down a brief sketch of rock climbing in Washington from the thirties to the eighties.

Although Northwest climbers like Jim Crooks, Art Winder and Joe Halliwax climbed numerous rocks in the thirties, most of the climbs made prior to World War II didn't exactly fit our current conception of rock climbing. The earliest climbers generally climbed only on rock when it was necessary to reach the summit of a peak. Viewing rock climbing as a necessary difficulty en route to a greater end, these early climbers left it to the next generation to seek out the technical difficulty of rock climbing as an end in itself. Ironically, the war had a significant impact on allowing this re-evaluation to occur.

During the war, the U.S. Army's 10th Mountain Division trained a number of climbers in new techniques, and by the war's end it had made available a great deal of equipment, such as pitons and nylon ropes. The postwar climbers first used these techniques and items of equip-ment on the many magnificent, unclimbed peaks in Wash-ington, thus avoiding the lowland areas for the most part. Nevertheless, a new trend in climbing was beginning.

In the late forties, pinnacles, especially those in the Stuart Range, became the rage. Because these all require fairly long and difficult approaches, the stage was set for rock climbing for its own sake. The seminal event was the first ascent of Midway on Castle Rock, which occurred after Wes Grande and Jack Kendricks noticed a prominent line up the center of the face. Their great interest in the climb was due largely to the short approach; a short approach is often considered one of the hallmarks of modern rock climbing. It took several attempts before Grande, Fred Beckey and Jack Schwabland, using fixed ropes and aid because of the dirt-filled cracks, finally succeeded.

Fred Beckey was the leader of this postwar generation. Not the premier technical climber of his day, he more than compensated for this through his tireless explorations. In this day of few unclimbed peaks, no climber in the world will probably equal the variety of Beckey's first-ascent record. In the Cascades, he will best be remembered for pioneering mountain climbs, but he has also been a major figure in the development of all three areas covered in this guide. Other climbers active in the postwar era include Grande, Schwabland, Dick Widrig, Joe Hieb, Don Wilde and Pete Schoening.

The ease of approaches, along with constantly improving equipment and techniques, pushed standards higher and higher. Climbers in the forties and fifties still considered Leavenworth a practice area, so it was left to the next generation to bring rock climbing to the front as a sport in its own right. A look at the first-ascent records indicate that 1957 was the beginning of serious rock climbing in Washington. Prior to that time, the four major crags of the Leavenworth area—Castle, Midnight, Snow Creek Wall and Peshastin—had only a handful of lines. In the mid-sixties, by the time the technically oriented climbers of the late fifties had moved on, over a hundred climbs had been recorded. Index was also visited for the first time, and several Grade IV routes on the Upper Wall were climbed.

In the late fifties and early sixties, aid climbing was the hallmark of a serious climber. The most active people began to do more and more intimidating lines, often including bivouacs, but the Northwest was still well below other areas in the country in technical rock climbing. On the other hand, the members of this group, including Fred Beckey, Dave Beckstead, Eric Bjornstad, Pat Callis, Ed Cooper, Dan Davis, Don Gordon, Dick McGowan and Jim Stuart, were, along with the Teton regulars, the best mountaineers in the country. Moreover, although aid climbing was of great interest to many people, the climbers in this group did not avoid free climbing. As good mountaineers realize, free climbing is usually the quickest and most efficient method. Though their alpine orientation often defined the style of the day, if it was more efficient to use aid, they used aid. Nevertheless, the climbers of this group did free climb some impressive sections of rock, a couple of which are currently rated 5.10. Then the next generation, intensely interested in rock climbing as pure sport, moved in.

In 1964, Bill Marts came to Seattle and took over the University of Washington climbing program, an act that was to have far-reaching consequences. Marts had climbed in Colorado with Layton Kor and company and was successful in relating his enthusiasm to his students; among them were Jim Madsen, Tom Hargis, John Marts, and Phil Leatherman.

In 1966, Hargis and Madsen took their first trip to Yosemite, the place where granite techniques were being pushed, a fact not yet appreciated by the somewhat isolated Northwest climbers. Hargis stayed the longest and returned with a wondrous new technique for climbing cracks called jamming. He spent three hours on Castle Rock's Damnation Crack demonstrating to an assembled group that cracks could be used for more than protection. The stage was now set for Washington's free climbing "Golden Era." The activists included Jock McPherson, Ron Burgner, Del Young and Fred Stanley, but no one took it to heart more than Jim Madsen.

Madsen was a six-foot-four, 210-pound football player whose strength and enthusiasm surpassed even his size. His style, imitated by many Northwest climbers of the day, was to work himself into a rage and then attack. Madsen's

Northwest contributions are tremendous; he singled out most everything in sight and attempted them free. A majority of the classic Midnight lines fell to him, as well as a number of routes at Castle, Snow Creek Wall and Peshastin. Like almost all Northwest climbers, he was an alpinist as well as a rock climber, but it's for his rock climbing that he will be remembered. On October 16, 1968, the 21-year-old Madsen rappelled down El Capitan attempting to help storm-bound friends. While they were all right, Madsen rappelled off the end of his rope, tragically ending his meteoric career. Royal Robbins said of Madsen: "[His] marriage of passion, energy, strength and discipline bordered on the inconceivable. He was the stuff of which heroes are made."[1]

Madsen's death stunned Northwest rock climbers. The question became: what now? The answer was to keep moving forward, to repeat the routes and to discover new ones. Al Givler kept the spirit alive more than others, but Mark Weigelt, Mead Hargis and Jim Langdon were also of great importance. Many others, including Bruce Albert, Ron Burgner, Pete Doorish, Heinz Graupe, Jim McCarthy, John Marts, Thom Nephew, Jay Ossiander, Bill Sumner, Pat Timson and Del Young, were also very active. A look at the first-ascent list could lead one to the conclusion that little was done, but that supposition is far from the truth. The group repeated the Madsen routes, breaking a psychological barrier that may have been more difficult than that Madsen faced in making the first free ascents. After all, just because Madsen could do it didn't mean anyone else could. In the late sixties and early seventies, this group proved the routes were possible; and indeed, with a bit of experience, some were even reasonable.

Another important rediscovery of the time was Icicle Canyon. Although climbers had paid perfunctory attention to this canyon before, now they did dozens of routes; yet in keeping with a tradition that still largely exists today, few of these climbs were formally recorded. It is not uncommon

[1]Royal Robbins, "In Memoriam: James Thomas Madsen, 1947-1968," *American Alpine Journal*, Vol. 16, No. 2, (1969) pp. 496-497.

to hike an hour or two up the hill to climb some obscure rock only to discover an ancient rappel sling at its top.

The post-Madsen generation also began to pay serious attention to the Index area. Jim Langdon added several difficult aid routes, while Mark Weigelt, Ron Burgner, Thom Nephew, Mead Hargis, Al Givler and others were involved with opening up the first 5.10 climbs.

In the late sixties, Darrington felt rock climbers for the first time. Fred Beckey discovered that a new logging road gave good access to the Witch Doctor Wall, so he assembled a party and established the area's first route. The next few years saw only a couple of lines added in spite of the area's potential. Most visitors returned with tales of green, never noticing the oceans of white rock between.

Probably the reason the post-Madsen generation left little tangible evidence of their efforts in the Northwest can be traced to the obsession with Yosemite. Virtually all the area's best climbers spent long periods of time in the Valley. Upon return, it seemed boring to do the same old routes again, and new ones seemed tame and dirty in comparison to El Cap and the rest.

As is always the case, younger climbers were coming up, and they wanted their new routes. Influenced by Saturday night get-togethers in the Icicle with the slightly older climbers, this bunch continued many of the same sort of activities: mountain climbs, hard route repeats, Icicle routes and Valley jaunts with the occasional new routes. Bruce Carson and Dave Anderson added the most new routes. Carson, in particular, led the way in all-nut ascents and solo, big-wall climbs; Pat Timson and Don Harder led many difficult free climbs in all areas; and Brent Hoffman and Karl Kaiyala virtually made the Upper Town Wall their private playground due to a lack of interest by most other parties. Don Brooks, usually accompanied by Hoffman, began the first systematic exploration of Darrington. Other important figures of the time included Steve Barnett, Julie Brugger, Rich Carlstad, Bob Crawford, Dave Davis, Pete Doorish, Carla Firey, Cal Folsum, Katherine Freer, Donn Heller, Don Leonard, Rick LeDuc, Greg Markov and Jim McCarthy.

By the mid-seventies, most of the serious climbers had moved on to other areas and pursuits, as had the climbers before them. Almost all the late-sixties' to mid-seventies' climbers are still active, but few seem to rock climb in Washington on any regular basis.

New pressures started building in the early seventies that had to do mainly with overpopulation and the rising level of ecological awareness. Where only a relatively small group had been active, the floodgates were now open as more people discovered the pleasure and excitement of climbing. During this time, pitons were still being used by conservative climbers and those lacking the knowledge and experience to safely use clean-climbing devices. With the climbing popularity of the mid-seventies, routes that had initially seen a few aid ascents followed by dozens of free, nut ascents were beginning to be aided again with all the attendant damage to the rock. Tempers often ran high as ethical discussion flared. With the advent of more information, such as the 1976 Leavenworth and Index guide and numerous articles in climbing publications, the issues have largely been sorted out. Today, one rarely sees a piton on routes that have gone free, for climbers are not only testing new and old routes but preserving them for future generations as well.

The period from the mid-seventies to 1978 can be described as the "doldrums." The apprentice training system had largely broken down, so new climbers basically had to start from scratch and push their own way. This new beginning had a highly beneficial effect, for a number of superb climbers developed, largely free of the intimidations of having to follow older, more experienced climbers. A group led by Paul Boving that included Matt and Jamie Christiansen, Bob McDougall, Steve Pollack, Resse Martin and Kjell Swedin established several outstanding lines. Another group, including Duane Constantino, Chris Greyell, Dave Tower and Dave Whitelaw, had Darrington to themselves. With occasional others, the Darrington group established over 80 new pitches, by far the greatest new route output in some time. The impressive achievements of these groups and others, however, went largely unknown, since there was very little communication among groups.

The last few years have been the most intense in Northwest climbing history in terms of the number of different climbers establishing new routes. There are now more talented climbers than ever before seriously seeking out new climbs. Many short routes take several days due to the need for cleaning, but these disagreeable tasks pose no obstacle to this newest generation of climbers. Jim Yoder is largely responsible for the development of new routes on Castle Rock, while Kjell Swedin and Bob McDougall deserve credit for the same on Midnight. Swedin, Mc-Dougall, Dan Lepeska and Don Brooks have added a number of new lines at Index. Pat Timson made the long-awaited ascent of Midnight's Supercrack. Doug Klewin, Rick Graham, Pat and Dan McNerthney, Bob Plumb and Paul Christiansen have also added new routes throughout the Leavenworth area. Apart from extreme routes and those requiring a tremendous amount of cleaning, new routes are getting harder to come by, but great potential for exploration exists in all areas.

Look up Tumwater or Icicle Canyons or around Index and Darrington; untouched rock abounds where you can pick a line and try it. Many of the routes you choose, however, may previously have been climbed even though no traces have been left behind. Share your finds with others, but don't fall into the trap that many do in thinking that "my friends and I are the first really hard-core bunch around this area." As we enter the eighties, the lines are drawn. An ever-increasing commitment on the part of the leading climbers will forge the way for the climbing population as a whole. Everyone will undoubtedly benefit.

RATINGS

The venerable Yosemite Decimal System is used in this guide. Washington routes, particularly those at Leavenworth, have been traditionally underrated when compared to areas in California, where the system was developed. In light of this, efforts have been made to standardize the areas. Many climbers have participated in a rating survey, but no one should regard any rating as absolute. Many new routes have had only a few ascents and are thus in question. Even routes that have had hundreds of ascents provoke spirited arguments when the subject of ratings is brought up.

In brief, the system is divided into overall grades I through VI based on difficulties encountered, time involved and the overall seriousness of the climb. Grade I or II routes most commonly require only a short period of time. A grade III will usually take a competent party much of the day in good weather. A grade IV will often take all day, and for slower climbers may require a bivouac. Grade V climbs usually require a bivouac for all but the fastest parties. No grade VI routes are currently within the scope of this book.

Following the overall grade is the rating of the most difficult free move. All climbs listed here fall into the fifth-class range, the class where ropes, protection and carabiners are routinely used. The higher the second number— 5.6, 5.7 and so on—the more difficult the climb. Letter subdivisions have been added to the upper grades in order to further delineate the difficulties. Some see this as nit-picking, but the difference between 5.10a and 5.10d is so pronounced that virtually everyone climbing at that standard is most interested in and aware of the distinctions indicated by the system. Routes in the 5.7 to 5.9 range are divided into two classes, those with a plus (+) and those without. Some 5.10 to 5.12 routes also divide into these two classes which means that in these cases no agreement has been reached regarding a letter subdivision.

A problem with ratings, especially in the higher grades, is the size differences in people. Everyone has a unique combination of height, reach, finger thickness, and the like, that may or may not be suited to a particular climb. A route featuring a long reach may be easy for a 6 footer and impossible for a shorter person, whereas a 5½ footer with thinner fingers may be exactly the right size for some thin crack routes. All climbers operating among the higher standards have failed on particular climbs solely for this reason.

Aid-climbing difficulties are expressed in a 0 to 5 system. If pitons are required, the number is preceded by the letter A. If the aid can be accomplished on nuts alone, the letter C (for chocks) precedes it. Climbs with an A0 rating require only an occasional aid move.

EQUIPMENT

The equipment needed in the areas covered here is the standard equipment used in all areas. Aid climbs, especially those in the Index area, require a heavy concentration of pitons in the knifeblade-to-baby-angle range. When a route description suggests carrying a rack to a certain size, nuts from small wires up to the indicated size should be included. The size of the rack depends on an individual party's preference and experience within each area. New routes often require wire brushes, bush clippers, digging tools and other such implements. The standard rope length is 150 feet, but some may find 165 feet occasionally useful. As in most rock areas, helmets are not often worn, but the difficulties involved with rescue, the occasional loose rock, and the likelihood of another party somewhere above often make wearing helmets a most sensible practice.

Equipment, no matter now good, should not be implicitly trusted. This is especially true of fixed pitons, bolts and rappel setups. Judgment that can only be gained through experience must be exercised at every moment on every climb.

ETHICS

The burning ethical questions of the sixties and seventies seem to have fallen by the wayside in the practical eighties. Never an ethical hotbed like Colorado, Washington has seen climbing styles deteriorate further and further. This isn't the place, however, to debate questions of style.

Of greater concern now is the use of anything that destroys the rock. The main culprits here are pitons, whether used for protecting free climbs or for aid. It is hard to believe that people still nail Angel Crack or the Index Slab routes; unfortunately, it does happen occasionally. Perhaps it is a reaction against wilderness preservation, a desire to proceed unrestricted, or simply ignorance. It should be remembered that these climbs will be here for many years; pin scars, broken flakes and other damage definitely reduce the esthetic qualities of climbs for generations to come.

Difficult questions are raised by the use of pitons for aid on routes that have gone free. It is accepted practice throughout the English-speaking world that once someone has successfully done a climb free, others will no longer use aid on that particular route. A wide enough variety of aid climbs are available throughout the state that one should respect the achievements of others and the integrity of the rock itself by refraining from further damaging the climbs.

The practice of adding bolts to existing free climbs is absolutely unjustifiable, except in rare cases. A good example is the West Face Direct at Peshastin. This difficult climb is often top roped but rarely led due to the lack of protection. Another bolt would make it a completely different climb; it is better for climbers to raise their standards than to bring the climb down to their level. One exception to this rule is when the active climbers collectively agree, usually after a year or two of debate, to add a bolt for safety reasons. Few people disagree with the addition of a third belay bolt, especially at a place like Darrington, where climbs are often completely dependent on bolt placements.

In the eyes of some, chalk destroys the rock and the beauty of the experience. Time has shown that most chalk does wash off, but especially in the summer, it may be weeks or months between cleansing storms. People will undoubtedly continue the practice, but they should exercise moderation. Chalking up to belay is definitely unnecessary.

Key to topo drawings:

X	**Bolt**
F.P.	**Fixed pin**
①	**Pitch number**
Ⓐ	**Route designation**
⌀	**Rappel point**
H.B.	**Hanging belay**

DARRINGTON

The Darrington climbing area lies largely in the Clear and Copper Creek drainage above the community of Darrington. The western approach is via State Highway 530, reached from Interstate 5 or State Highway 9, north of Everett and south of Mount Vernon. Other approaches are from the north, via State Highway 17A or from the south via the Mountain Loop Highway.

To reach the climbing area, head east through town; drive straight when the main road turns 90 degrees; take the forced right, then turn left onto the Sauk River Road. In less than three miles, road 3210 angles right, just after a bridge where the road changes from pavement to gravel. In some five miles it branches again, left to Exfoliation Dome or right to Three O'Clock Rock, The Comb and Green Giant Buttress.

Darrington (D-Town), is the most recently discovered and least-developed area covered in this book. Manuel Gonzales, one of the first climbers in the area, wrote that the "soundness of the rock and its proximity to Seattle should contribute to the future popularity of the area."[2] Strangely enough, this prophecy has yet to be borne out, especially to the few climbers intimately familiar with the place. One can only speculate that the lack of publicity (at least prior to Fred Beckey's 1976 *Darrington and Index Rock Climbing Guide*), the often poor weather, the moss and dirt, and the occasionally frightening lack of protection have kept people away. This era of neglect is rapidly coming to an end as people discover the many virtues of the area, primarily its relative remoteness and its unique face/slab climbing.

Five major walls lie within the area, two of them on the only peak in this guide, Exfoliation Dome. Witch Doctor Wall, the largely hidden side of Exfoliation, contains the guide's longest aid lines as well as one surprising free line up the center of the face. The other side of

---

[2]Manuel A. Gonzales, "Darrington Walls," *American Alpine Journal*, Vol. 17, No. 2, (1971), pp. 345-346.

Exfoliation Dome, Blueberry Hill, currently has four completed routes of varying natures. At the head of the Copper Creek drainage, the Green Giant Buttress does little to live up to its intimidating title, having several outstanding, long free climbs. The many-buttressed Comb is the least-developed cliff, due perhaps to the rough nature of the approach trail. Finally, Three O'Clock Rock, the area's most-developed crag, contains approximately half of the current routes, due in part to an easy approach and comparatively short routes.

D-Town free routes, especially those on the last three crags mentioned, contain features that are largely unique to Washington and present some special problems. The major one results from the fact that many of these climbs follow fantastic, randomly located knobs rather than crack systems and are thus bolt protected. Because it is exhausting, unesthetic and expensive to place bolts, most people have drilled the minimum number possible. Therefore some of the routes may require 50-foot runouts between protection. These runouts, in turn, can make the distantly spaced bolts extremely difficult to locate, causing route-finding problems. Another potential problem worth mentioning, especially for those who wander off route, is the occasional lichen and moss on the rock. A common solution is for the leader to include a small wire brush on the rack.

It's necessary to differentiate between unprotected and long runouts. A route that is rated 5.10 will generally have the crux moves well protected, but may have 5.8 moves far from the last bolt or nut. To a 5.10 climber this would probably be merely a long runout, but 5.8 climbers attempting to push their standards will undoubtedly find it extremely unprotected. Bolts are accurately marked on the topos in this book, so prospective climbers should be able to estimate these intangible difficulties before launching out. Climbers should not be tempted to carry bolt kits on existing routes, for each climb is finished, a work reflecting the standards and style of its creators; as such, the routes should be appreciated. Those wishing better-protected climbs are invited to seek out new lines of their own, keeping in mind that long runouts tend to be accepted in this type of climbing.

Darrington climbers are frequently challenged to arrange nut placements behind fragile flakes or shallow corners. Small wired nuts, often of the single-cable variety, as well as numerous runners will often prove useful. Another convenient piece of equipment is a belay seat for the many semi-hanging belays. Virtually all Darrington routes require rappel descents. Two 150-foot ropes and adequate sling material should be carried on all routes.

Good route finding, delicate balance, occasional steel nerves and sensational knob trotting — they're all called for in this exciting area.

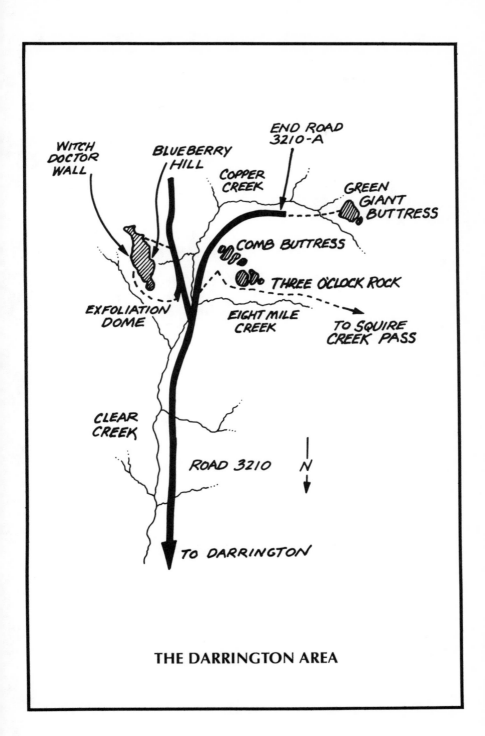

WITCH DOCTOR WALL

BLUEBERRY HILL

COPPER CREEK

END ROAD 3210-A

GREEN GIANT BUTTRESS

COMB BUTTRESS

THREE O'CLOCK ROCK

EXFOLIATION DOME

EIGHT MILE CREEK

TO SQUIRE CREEK PASS

CLEAR CREEK

ROAD 3210

N

TO DARRINGTON

THE DARRINGTON AREA

THREE O'CLOCK ROCK

Below Three O'Clock Rock, Squire Pass Trail begins. A half-hour to one-hour walk up this trail—the only good one in the climbing area—is the base of the routes. Shortly after breaking out of the trees below the rock, a steep scramble up a rough trail leads through the willows to the base of the Big Tree area. Continuing on the main trail takes one to the North Buttress as well as to the pass.

The North Buttress sports four routes at the present time. Bushy Galore is the obvious bush-filled corner just left of center. Rubber Soul uses a dike, faintly visible to the left. Silent Running and Beanberry Delight are to the right.

The South Buttress is approached from the North Buttress by scrambling along the rock's base or from the scramble trail. The Big Tree starts, all from a wide crack, are obvious. The Kone and Cornucopia are easiest to approach by scrambling up the first trees left of the Big Tree starts. Farther left, the Tidbits line is left of the large roofs. As the "trail" swings up a slight rise, the Rash will be visible as a great swath of knobs 75 to 150 feet up. A short, brushy walk around the now-curving rock will lead to the Conan's Crack area. The Conan's climb is a long right-facing corner, the only one on Three O'Clock Rock. Frosted Flake is a small piece of rock partially hidden by trees.

Three O'Clock is unique in Darrington in that the easy approach and relatively short climbs make it possible to do several in a day, thus providing a low-pressure, relaxing outing.

THREE O'CLOCK ROCK
F. Shot in the Dark
J. Tidbits
K. The Kone
N. Big Tree Two
P. Rubber Soul
R. Silent Running

THE CONAN'S AND RASH AREAS

A. URBAN PLOWBOY (not shown)
I, 5.8; nuts to 3" including many large ones

This is the left-facing dihedral 50 ft. left of the Frosted Flake. Rappel the route.

B. SHRIMPSIDE (not shown)
I, 5.7; small nuts

Left of Conan's Crack is the 30-ft. Frosted Flake. Move up to the Flake's left side by first scrambling to a belay ledge, then up a 5.6 pitch to a forest at the base of the Flake. Tiptoe up the stimulating left side to a 150-ft. rappel from the Flake's summit.

C. TRUNKLINE (not shown)
I, 5.9; nuts to 4"

On the right side of the Frosted Flake from the Shrimpside forest, traverse under the Flake to a jam through two trees.

D. THE PLAN (not shown)
II, 5.8; nuts to 2"

After one pitch of Conan's Crack, climb a short, flaring hand crack on the left, then another pitch to a belay under a block and finally over the block into the woods. Descend via rappel.

E. CONAN'S CRACK (not shown)
II, 5.8; nuts to 6"

This is the obvious right-facing corner. The final 10 ft. may be avoided by traversing right. The route is four pitches; descend via rappel.

F. SHOT IN THE DARK
II, 5.10 +; nuts to 3"

A couple of hundred feet left of Tidbits, several prominent curved cedars grow near the wall's base. Begin near these in a mossy arch, then run it out to a hidden bolt. Belay higher below a small roof, then cross the roof and belay under its larger relative. One more roof crossing and more face climbing lead to the finish. Rappel the route.

G. WHEN BUTTERFLIES KISS BUMBLEBEES
I. 5.8; nuts to 1"

Left of two 50-ft. dihedrals is a flake system leading up to a three-bolt belay. From this belay go up slightly right to cross a corner to a steep wall. Rappel the route from a bolt belay at the top of the pitch.

H. RASHIONALIZATION
I, 5.7; nuts to 3"

Face climb into the right-hand corner mentioned in Bees and Flies, then leave the corner to follow a ramp to the three-bolt belay. Shoot up the wild Rash, then traverse left until it's possible to continue up to a belay. Rappel the route.

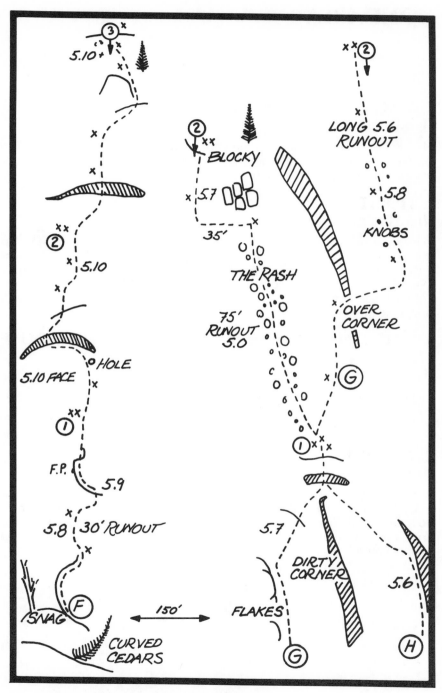

THREE O'CLOCK ROCK: RASH AREA

KONE AREA

I. MAGIC BUS (not shown)
II, 5.8

Shortly left of the Tidbits' dike, the trail begins to slope up. Start here; pass over a small roof, then belay on a ledge near some trees. Pass over the tree to an open book, then bear right for five more pitches to end above the Big Tree.

J. TIDBITS
II, 5.10b; nuts to 1"

Left of the massive roofs are a number of trees. It is easy to scramble up through these, but the original line is more sporting. A small dike on the right edge of a smooth slab leads to a bolt belay. Climb up through a narrow trough, over a roof and up the Crescent Crack to a belay. Another pitch leads up the "A" past many bolts. One more pitch leads to the top and the descent back down the route.

K. THE QUIN KONEHEAD PRE-MEMORIAL ROUTE (THE KONE)
II, 5.9; nuts to 1"

Right of the roofs and left of the Cornucopia flake is a white slab. Two pitches travel straight up this slab before angling left under a long roof. The final pitch reaches the Tidbits' summit. Rappel Tidbits.

L. CORNUCOPIA
II, 5.9+; nuts to 3"

A long, flake pitch ends on a pedestal. Pass a bolt, cross a roof and corner to a belay 15 ft. right of The Kone's second pitch. Pass one more bolt, then angle 30 ft. left to a hidden line of bolts between the Dick's Demise corner and the Kone roof. One more short pitch leads to the Big Tree. Descend via the Big Tree Rappel Route.

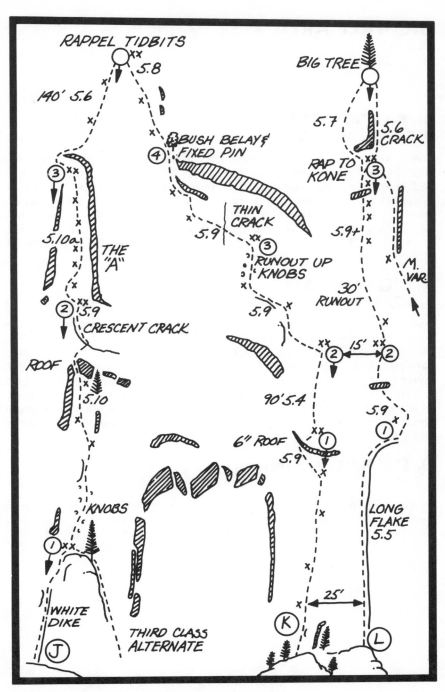

THREE O'CLOCK ROCK: KONE AREA

BIG TREE AREA

M. BIG TREE ONE
II, 5.7, A1; nuts to 3"

Shortly after emerging from the trail, you will see an obvious wide, low-angle crack as an island in an ocean of moss. Take this crack to a ledge filled with cedar trees. Next, move up right of the bushes and climb around a large roof, then back left on a horizontal crack to a tree belay. A 75-ft. pitch follows the corner to a bolt and a horn. One is then confronted with two shallow, left-facing corners. Follow the right corner up past a bolt to the Big Tree. Variation: DICK'S DEMISE. II, 5.7. At the final Big Tree One belay, take the left of the two corners.

N. BIG TREE TWO
II, 5.7; nuts to 3"

From the cedar-filled ledge, one pitch up Big Tree One, angle right over several dihedrals to belay from a sturdy tree. The next obvious pitch is somewhat unprotected and leads to one of the ubiquitous D-Town, semi-hanging belays. The original route goes from here up the arch to the only bolt initially placed on the route. A variation is to avoid the arch by aiming for a system to its left. Both paths join and lead up easier climbing to a short left-facing corner and the pedestal belay at its top. The final, easy pitch drops down and traverses over to the Big Tree and the start of the excellent rappel route.

O. THE JINX (not shown)
I, 5.9

From the Divide, a bolt protects face moves up the left wall to a prominent layback crack. When the crack arches, move straight up the face to a prominent roof. Cross the roof to a belay 15 ft. higher. Rappel the route.

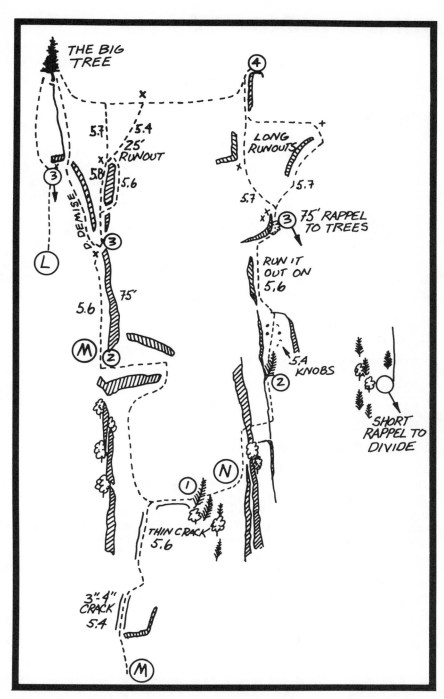

THREE O'CLOCK ROCK: BIG TREE AREA

THE NORTH BUTTRESS

P. RUBBER SOUL
II, 5.8; nuts to 1½"

About 50 ft. left of the Bushy Galore dihedral is a vertically trending dike. Begin on the Galore line and angle left to a crescent-shaped ledge. Cross a stepped roof and continue up the dike to a large cedar bush under a roof. Angle right to a broken area on the Galore route which is then rappelled.

Q. BUSHY GALORE (not shown)
III, 5.7; nuts to 2"

This is the prominent grassy dihedral starting several pitches above the base of the rock. It is recommended to rappel after five pitches, making the route a grade II; but it is possible to continue up five more pitches to the top.

R. SILENT RUNNING
II, 5.9; nuts to 2"

Scramble up to a ledge below a small roof some 100 ft. above the ground. Cross over this roof, then follow bolts for two pitches. The third pitch passes a bolt, then runs it out to a small pinnacle. The final pitch goes up to a roof and then exits right, off the cliff. A double rope rappel down the route is possible after the second pitch.

S. BEANBERRY DELIGHT
II, 5.8; nuts to 1"

Three hundred feet above the toe of the rock is the upper of two cedar bushes. This is reached directly, third to minimal fifth class, or by angling 150 ft. left to a ledge with a small maple, then aiming right for the cedar. Next, go fairly straight to the fourth bolt on the Silent Running route, then right under a small roof, back left over it, and finally up to a cedar bush. Another pitch angles up and right to a dihedral on the right side of the buttress. Easy climbing leads up 150 ft. to the start of the rappel route. Variation, 5.9: From the first tree belay, move right on the ledge, then up an odd crack. A long runout leads to a roof. Belay just above on wired nuts (long pitch). Move up and left to the Silent Running belay.

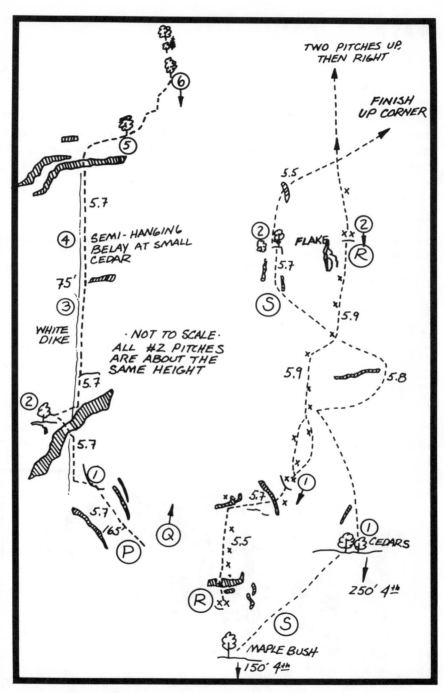

THREE O'CLOCK ROCK: NORTH BUTTRESS

THE COMB

The approach to The Comb begins at the base of Three O'Clock Rock. Start below several silver-trunked trees near Magic Bus and follow a rough trail to the extreme right edge of the rock. Once at the base, Bump City will show as a steep, knob-covered wall just left of a white dike. Farther on, the trail requires a short down climb after which the short Barrington's Revenge will come into view. Skyrider lies on this same buttress, just right of a huge gully.

A. SKYRIDER
II, 5.10a; nuts to 3"

Skyrider's second pitch is most easily recognized as the major right-facing dihedral on a wall dominated by left-facing corners. The first pitch ends at a belay from big nuts partway up the crack. From the next belay, on a ramp, finish via tree rappels.

B. BARRINGTON'S REVENGE
I, 5.7; nuts to 1½"

Barrington's is easily identified as the only 30-ft. crack with a down-climb descent on the left side.

C. BUMP CITY
I, 5.8; nuts to 1"

This climb may be somewhat difficult to locate. Key features include a white dike, a fairly steep, knobby wall and a short ¾-in. horizontal crack just off the ground. Belay from bushes.

THE COMB

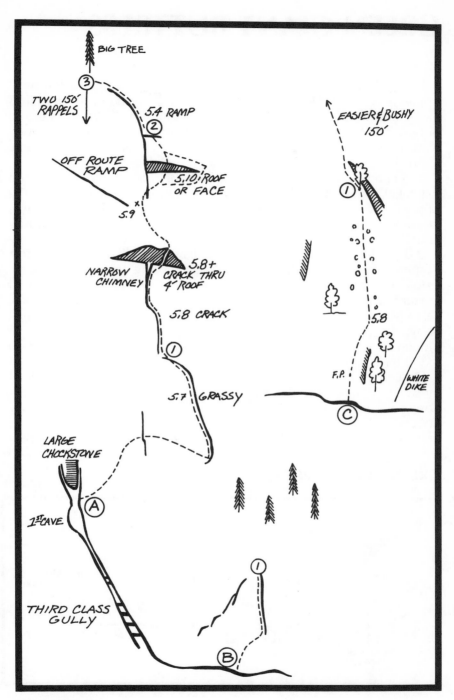

THE COMB

GREEN GIANT BUTTRESS

Lying at the head of the Copper Creek Valley is one of the most impressive walls in Washington, the Green Giant Buttress. The cliff's name and those of the first two routes done on it, Avoidance and Botany 101, give scant clues as to the outstanding climbing here. Newer routes with names like Dreamer and The Fast Lane tend to give a more accurate picture.

The climbs are fairly easy to spot from the road. Avoidance, on the left, takes the giant gully/dihedral system partway up before traversing out to the left. Botany 101 takes a dihedral system farther right and less prominent than that of Avoidance but still quite distinctive. Dreamer and The Fast Lane lie on either side of the Botany line.

Woe to those who fail to locate the trail as they will be entering into a desperate battle. From the car, take care, ignoring new logging marks, to locate an old trail through the woods. The trail is fairly obvious until the turn to the usually dry creek bed is reached. A cairn may or may not be in place here, but in any case, three low-angled waterfalls lie just above this point. Probe carefully in the jungle to the right to locate a hidden creek bed; once you find it, it's easy to follow the creek bed up to the base of the climbs.

Descent is, as usual, by rappel. Avoidance rappels off the left side of the wall; all other routes rappel off right. From Botany's finish, walk down a gully until it is time to begin rappelling. This will vary depending on the individual. Some down climb far enough to need only two rappels, while others start quite high and require five rappels.

GREEN GIANT APPROACH

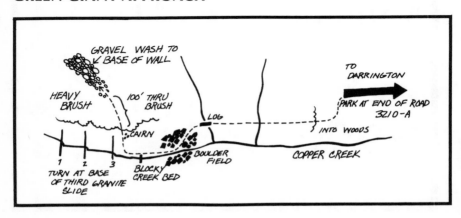

GREEN GIANT BUTTRESS
D. Dreamer
G. The Fast Lane

A. AVOIDANCE (not shown)
III, 5.8; nuts to 2"

This is the obvious gully/chimney on the left half of the wall. High up, avoid a spectacular chimney that ends in a dirt-choked crack by moving left to a tree-covered ridge. Cracks lead to easier ground, then into the woods. Rappel off left and bushwhack back.

B. TAKE THE RUNOUT
II, 5.10; nuts to 1½"

Scramble up to where Avoidance steepens. A 100-ft. pitch leads to a belay at a curving roof. Climb under the roof, traverse right 80 ft. with scant protection, then do a body fall to bushes on the Dreamer route.

C. THE GIANT'S TEARS
II, 5.10+, A0; nuts to 2"

After a pitch of the Runout, pass several bolts (one aid bolt); cross the Runout, then continue up past many bolts to join Dreamer.

D. DREAMER
IV, 5.9; nuts to 3"

Start at the Botany 101 dihedral; angle left and up on small ledges and cracks to a belay beneath a prominent crack. The next belays are above the crack in some bushes, then in a small dihedral. Next, angle left past bolts to a narrow ledge. A pitch up cracks ends at a cedar where face climbing leads to a roof. Undercling this roof, then move right to enter the Blue Crack. Travel left under the next roof, then step over it to testy face climbing. A knob pitch just right of the bushy corner leads to a belay at this corner's finish. Step left to another knobby wall and another cedar belay. A final, short pitch reaches the knife-edge ridge crest.

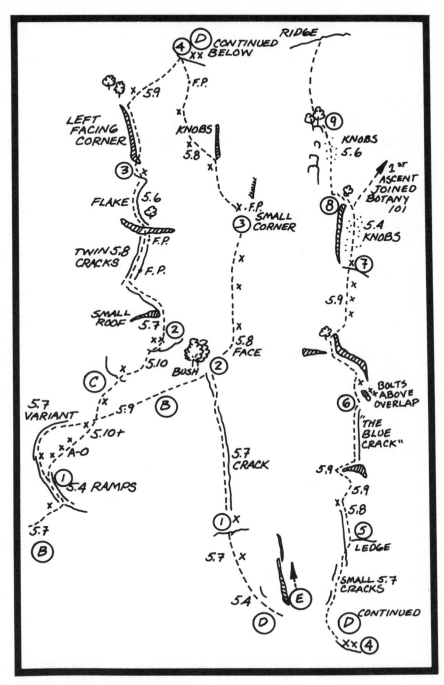

GREEN GIANT BUTTRESS

E. BOTANY 101 (partially shown)
III, 5.8; nuts to 3"

This obvious climb contains several 5.8 sections and up to ten pitches depending on how much is belayed at the start.

F. LOST IN SPACE
II, 5.10a; nuts to 2"

After approximately 450 ft. of Botany, gain a flat ledge, still in the corner. A pitch up flakes leads to the obvious finger crack above. From its finish, either join The Fast Lane or rappel the route.

G. THE FAST LANE
IV, 5.10c, A3; nuts to 2" (many small) plus eight pitons from two knifeblades to a ½" angle

Near the Botany start is a prominent, blocky flake. Climb past three bolts on a smooth face to a belay next to overlapping cracks. Move left to a belay on a vertical flake. Next, thread trees via the Isthmus of Rock, then move up to a bolt belay on top of a pedestal. After facing the Greyellian Rib, surge up a crack to a mossy ledge. From the left side of this ledge, move left around the crest of the rib to gain cracks leading to a belay below a large roof. The sixth pitch moves right around the roof via cracks, then uses two aid moves to regain the crest. Cracks and roofs on the crest lead to a belay below the final, difficult pitch of the route. A 40-ft., thin crack is nailed to where a lessening angle permits freeing into some trees. Two more fourth-class pitches complete the route.

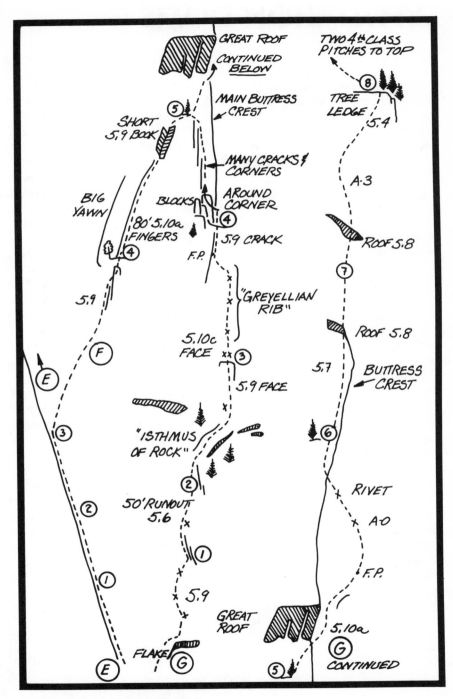

GREEN GIANT BUTTRESS

EXFOLIATION DOME

The first written reference to Darrington as a climbing area was by Fred Beckey who described Witch Doctor Wall as the "East Flank of the NW Spur of Helena Peak, the spur simply marked 4235." He also called it "quite possibly the most difficult 4000' summit in the state."[3] Few of those faced with the multiple free or aid pitches and the numerous rappels would disagree.

All routes, on both sides of Exfoliation Dome, when combined with the difficult descents are full-day or multi-day adventures on a mountain peak and as such should not be taken lightly. Normal mountaineering precautions, such as flashlights, rain gear and emergency bivouac equipment should be carried. Be prepared to spend the night, for it's a poor idea to attempt a descent of the Dome in the dark.

Witch Doctor Wall is fairly difficult to approach, because there is no trail. About a half mile after road 3210 branches, an old logging spur angles back left up the hill. Hike this short distance, then follow the creek bed, always staying right at junctions. Wet slabs, vegetation and talus regulate the speed at which one can move, so it is best to plan on one or two hours for the approach. A trail would be most welcome here.

Descent from the Dome can be a problem; there are many choices, but none is particularly attractive. At least five descents have been used, each with its own drawbacks. Although the most common route is down trees on the West Slabs, many return from this descent saying "never again." An excellent route is in place down the 23rd Psalm, but it can be difficult to locate from above. To reach the Psalm, head down the overlaps, feeling perhaps like you're walking off the edge of the world, until a set of runners appears; ten 150-ft. rappels follow. If this descent is chosen, a hammer and a bolt or two should be carried. The wooded buttress north of the Psalm and the North Ridge have also been used, but are not recommended. The descent requiring the least rappelling comes down the Witch Doctor side, far uphill from the routes. Some 100 feet south of the summit block, on the ridge above the finish of The West Slab, is a takeoff point for three rappels to the ground. This choice leaves one faced with the long walk around the Dome, a walk which may take up to two hours. The advantage of this

---

[3]Fred Beckey, "Witch Doctor Wall," *American Alpine Journal*, Vol. 17, No. 1, (1971) p. 118.

last route in bad weather is that it allows one to get off the peak and into the woods fairly quickly; furthermore, it avoids descending the Granite Sidewalk which can become treacherous in wet weather.

Once at the base of the Witch Doctor Wall, it is fairly easy to locate the routes. The Checkered Demon is probably the guide's most obvious line. Sunday Cruise could be termed a variation of the Demon. The Witch Doctor Route passes through several large white scars, and finally, Thunder Road utilizes cracks just right of a fairly prominent, bushy dihedral.

The Blueberry Hill side of Exfoliation Dome bears little resemblance to the Witch Doctor Wall face. The approach, while not entirely simple, is at least straightforward. The climbs are quite variable; slabs, faces, cracks, aid and trees are all found. The descent is unfortunately the same as previously mentioned in the Witch Doctor introduction. One undesirable facet of Blueberry is that this wall has been observed to be geologically active from the buttress to the ridge. Helmets would provide little protection against some of the rock avalanches that have been spotted, but these avalanches can't be considered normal.

To approach these climbs, drive quite close to the Granite Sidewalk, then take this long tongue of rock up to the base of The West Slab. The North Ridge is best approached by following the Sidewalk, then traversing under the main face. The buttress to the left of the 23rd Psalm has been climbed, but details are lacking. The other routes are fairly apparent and distinctive.

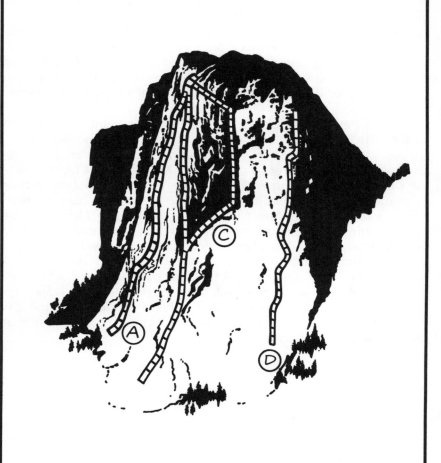

WITCH DOCTOR WALL
A. **The Witch Doctor Route**
C. **The Checkered Demon**
D. **Thunder Road**

WITCH DOCTOR WALL

A. THE WITCH DOCTOR ROUTE
V, 5.7, A3; 40 nuts and pitons from knifeblades to 2½"

This route takes a line between two prominent white scars, one a quarter of the way up, the other about two-thirds of the way up. A ledge is visible down and left from the first scar. Three pitches lead up flakes to the ledge's right side. From this good ledge, nail a thin crack to a large flake, then free climb to a belay spot. After a short bit of aid, tenuous free climbing leads to a cedar pitch. An aid pitch follows, leading to an alcove. Another tree pitch leads to Lunch Ledge. From Lunch's left side a hidden ramp leads up and right. The final, difficult pitch climbs a 5.7 crack followed by a short bit of aid. Scrambling leads to the top.

B. SUNDAY CRUISE
III, 5.9; nuts to 3" (many small)

Follow The Checkered Demon to the base of the Great Arch. This involves several hundred feet of third class followed by two fifth-class pitches up the left of two left-facing dihedrals. From a ledge below the Great Arch, traverse left to gain a dihedral and crack system; follow this system for three slightly left-trending crack pitches. Two more moderate pitches lead to the summit ridge.

C. THE CHECKERED DEMON
**V, 5.7, A3; 50 pitons and nuts from a RURP to 3", mostly
Lost Arrows**

Several hundred feet of third class lead to two fifth-class pitches up the left of two prominent left-facing dihedrals, which end at the base of the Great Arch. Three aid pitches with some A3 lead to the apex of the Arch where mixed free and aid climbing leads to another sling belay. More aid leads to a large, sloping platform. The last Demon pitch traverses left out of a dihedral to a cedar, then moves over to join the Witch Doctor Route for one more pitch.

D. THUNDER ROAD
IV, 5.6, A3; 25 pitons to 1½", mostly Lost Arrows, plus nuts

Several pitches of mixed climbing between two shallow, left-facing corners lead to a wandering pitch which ends at a hanging belay. One more aid pitch ends at a ledge below a distinctive dike. A pitch up a ramp leads to face cracks to the right of a bush-filled dihedral. Two difficult aid pitches up a left-facing corner lead to the top of the ridge.

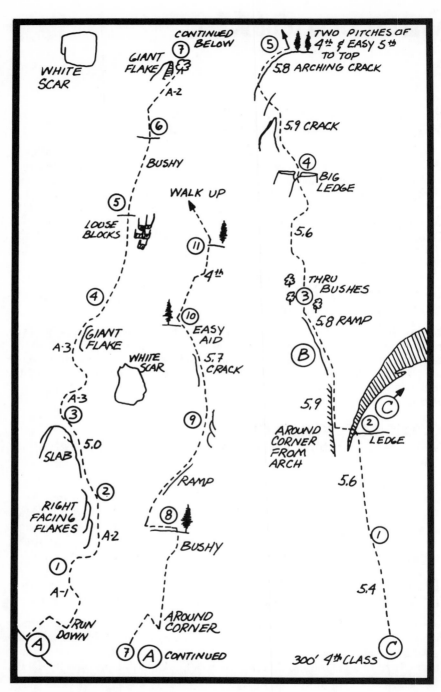

WITCH DOCTOR WALL

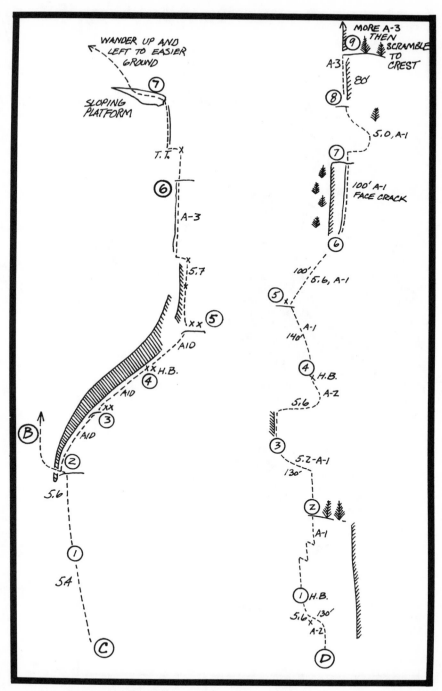

WITCH DOCTOR WALL

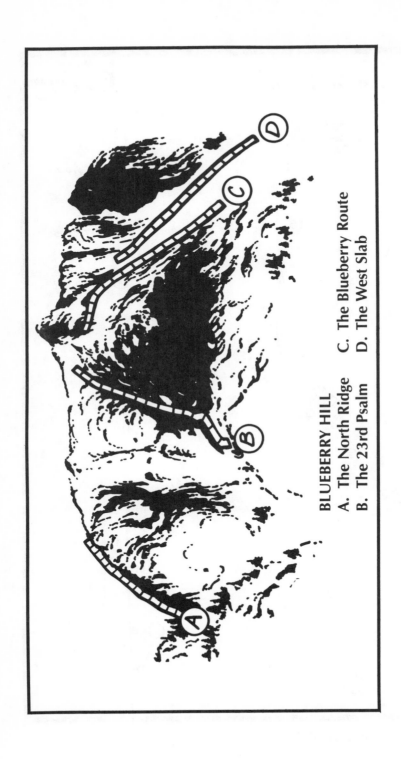

BLUEBERRY HILL

A. The North Ridge   C. The Blueberry Route
B. The 23rd Psalm   D. The West Slab

58

BLUEBERRY HILL

A. THE NORTH RIDGE
II, 5.7, A1; nuts to 1", plus several thin pitons

From the notch, climb the ridge, staying within 20 ft. of the left edge. Three belayed pitches with short sections of aid lead to scrambling.

B. THE 23rd PSALM
IV, 5.8, A3 +; 25 nuts and pins from RURPS to 2½"

Walk along the base of the wall to the large central depression. Third-class ramps lead up and right to the first belay. Continue another 150 ft., then up to a ledge. Nail over a roof to the Space Station Belay. Above lies a huge rock scar, fresh since the first ascent. There is some question regarding this section so be prepared. From a good ledge above the scar take the second dihedral system on the right to a belay horn. Bathooks lead up to where free climbing begins for five mid-fifth-class pitches.

C. THE BLUEBERRY ROUTE (WEST BUTTRESS)
III, 5.8; nuts to 2"

At the top of the Granite Sidewalk, a huge right-facing corner will be seen. The Blueberry route lies to the left of this system. Start with a fourth-class, wide crack and go to a ledge with a horn. The first fifth-class pitch moves up, then left then up to a cedar bush. Two pitches in a right-facing corner end out left, on a slab at the base of a wide crack, which is followed to the upper of two dead snags. Next, climb a thin crack, then traverse left to a large snag, then move up to a cedar bush. Easy slab climbing leads to a huge tree-covered ledge. A number of variations are possible off this ledge, starting anywhere from 30 to 75 yards left of the point of entry. All seem to involve one mid-fifth-class pitch, followed by several easy ones.

D. THE WEST SLAB
III, 5.8; nuts to 3"

At the top of the Granite Sidewalk, The West Slab lies just right of the buttress. After several hundred feet of fourth class, a pitch of broken rock leads to the base of smooth slabs. Pass a bolt, then make a long, unprotected traverse right to a shallow corner. At the top of the corner, move off the slab to broken rock. Climb up, traversing left above the roofs capping the slab, to rejoin the slab at a point where it has narrowed considerably. Two more rope lengths lead up to 400 ft. of broken fourth-class climbing, ending at a ridge crest. An easy ledge on the east side of the summit block leads to a short bit of scrambling.

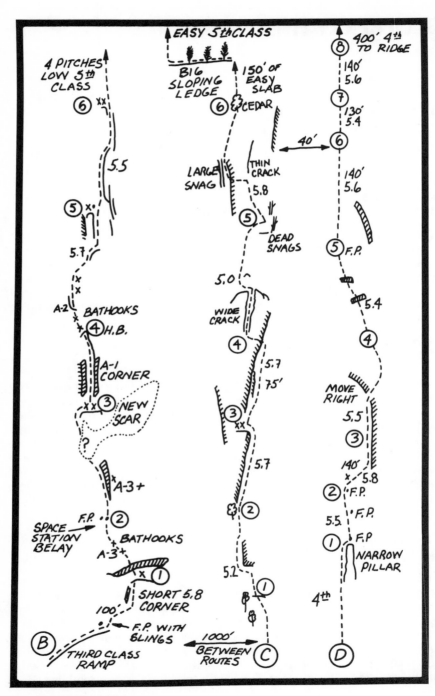

BLUEBERRY HILL

INDEX

Close to major population centers and very much in tune with the modern song of rock climbing, Index is an area just reaching maturity, yet it is an area promising to remain a vital climbing center in the Northwest for many years. Several widely traveled climbers have called Index the best place in the country to learn the difficulties of aid. Although the climbs are short compared to those of the other areas, their degree of complexity provides climbers with excellent opportunities to prepare for other big walls or simply to enjoy these climbs as ends in themselves. Because of the complexity and diversity of the climbs, Index has traditionally been the state's premier aid-climbing area, but now it is also becoming widely known for its superb crack climbing. While hundreds have free climbed on the friendly Slab with its moderately difficult routes, climbers are now undertaking the challenge of free climbing the steep routes throughout the area.

Apart from the low-angle Slab on the Lower Town Wall, Index is a very steep area, offering climbers the opportunity to get a great deal of air beneath their feet. The major problem here is the often poor weather and the resultant vegetation that chokes rarely climbed or unclimbed routes. A few hardy pioneers, however, are cleaning these. When their work is done, the Lower Town Wall especially will rank as one of the country's outstanding crags. Some argue it is in that class now.

The Upper Town Wall, site of the longer aid routes, has free-climbing opportunities as well, but they are more limited than the Lower Wall's. The areas below the Diamond route on the Upper Wall and the Lower Lump near the Lower Wall offer the greatest potential for new discoveries.

Problems may result from the trend to free old aid routes, thus limiting, in a strictly ethical sense, the number of existing aid possibilities. It should be stressed, however, that there are many routes on the easily approached Lower Wall which have limited free potential and which serve, therefore, as good aid practice. Other routes will eventually go free but can now be aided on nuts alone, thus limiting the destruction that pitons leave behind. Some of the routes that fall into these categories include: Snow White (first pitch), Numbah 10, 10% MV, Japanese Gardens, City Park (first pitch) and the Narrow Arrow Overhang. A climber who has done all of these is certainly technically ready for routes on the Upper Wall, Liberty Bell or many of the Yosemite classics.

Many small crags are scattered throughout the general Index area, but almost all of the climbing so far has been on the steep walls visible from the town. The areas are reached by leaving State Highway 2 and driving (or walking) into Index.

To find the Lower Wall, turn left at the school and continue along the river until reaching the wall. The Lower Lump is several hundred yards farther along the tracks. The Rattletale route is reached by parking near the school and bushwhacking to the start.

The Upper Wall has two approaches, one from town and one from logging roads above. The decision as to which approach to use should be based on experience with the area. The lower approach requires parking in town, then hiking up a rough trail to the base of the waterfall route. Parallel the railroad tracks, on foot, to a small, dirt parking lot with a water culvert where the steep 30- to 60-minute trail starts. Water is available at the base when the waterfall is running but its availability is questionable at other times. Once on top, either bushwhack left or locate a rough trail. Pass several large gullies, locate the rappel tree and follow this line back to the ground.

The upper approach is much easier if you're familiar with it and if you feel you'll succeed on your route. For the upper approach, 1¼ miles east of Goldbar leave U.S. 2 to turn onto Reiter Road. Follow this paved road for one mile before turning onto the gravel Trout Hatchery Road. Pass the hatchery, leave the main road (which ends at the Lower Wall) after three miles and continue uphill another three miles to a level forest road on the right. Once on this narrow lane, take the left branch and park at an old bridge. Because of the number of people here, especially in the upper area, climbers are cautioned not to leave valuables in their parked vehicles.

An easy, 15-minute walk, taking a left at the only junction, leads to the top of the wall. To the left (east), you'll find the end of the Davis-Holland route and the others beyond it. To the right, a scratch trail passes the Lamplighter route and leads to the rappel tree. If unsuccessful on a route, one can possibly outflank the wall on the west or climb back up the rappel gully (moderate fifth class). Still others leave a fixed line from the rappel tree to facilitate an easy return to the rim. Water will always be available at the bridge on the 15-minute trail.

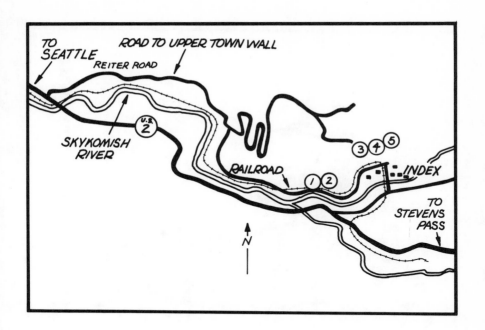

THE INDEX AREA

1. Lower Lump
2. Lower Town Wall
3. Upper Town Wall
4. The Cheeks
5. Diamond

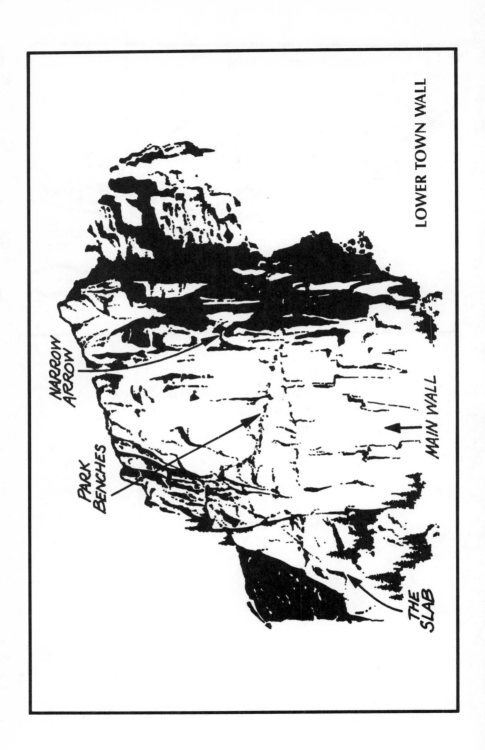

NARROW ARROW

PARK BENCHES

THE SLAB

MAIN WALL

LOWER TOWN WALL

LOWER TOWN WALL

The Lower Town Wall can be very confusing on first inspection, for it is one of the most crack-rich crags in the country. A few basic hints, however, should help straighten things out.

On the left edge is the comparatively low-angle Slab, bound on the left by the rotten Black Wall and on the right by the Main Wall. The Great Northern Route can be located by finding the Railroad Bolts (remnants of the quarrying era), which are visible from either the tracks or from below. These Bolts are beneath the slab with the double cracks. All other features can be located from these. It is possible to combine the short pitches in any number of combinations, but they are listed in such a manner as history, tradition and traffic-flow best suggest. Descent is best accomplished via rappel with either one or two ropes. With one rope, start from the large tree at the top and travel 75 feet down to the ring belay/rappel to the top of the Great Northern Slab. Another 75 feet leads to the Railroad Bolts where down climbing or one more rappel leads to the ground. Two ropes make it possible to go directly from the top to the Railroad Bolts.

The Roger's Corner route lies in and near the junction of the Slab and the Main Wall. Breakfast of Champions is slightly hidden behind a large fir on the steep wall above the Slab.

On the Main Wall, climbs in the Iron Horse route area should be evident after close inspection. Just right of the obvious corner and roof of the Sagittarius route, the 10% MV route starts. City Park route, a pin-scarred face crack about 50 feet right of 10%, cannot be mistaken for anything else.

The Narrow Arrow Overhang is the clean roof, one pitch above the ground. An excellent belay ledge on Narrow Arrow Direct route lies just right of this roof. The Pedestal, some 50 feet above the ledge, can be reached from the Park Bench East via some 5.6 climbing, giving access to the upper pitches of Narrow Arrow Direct to those wishing to avoid all traces of aid.

Buried Treasure route shares the first pitch of Narrow Arrow Direct to the Grey Snag before moving right, up an arch, to follow its own line to the Rotten Tree, just below the Narrow Arrow Summit. The Free at Last route starts in the shallow square chimney just down and right from the elegant Thin Fingers route.

Around the corner, the Quarry Crack route is visible as a wide crack on light-colored rock. The Narrow Arrow Pinnacle, a worthy goal, is most easily reached by starting up one of two 5.6 pitches on quarried rock. A chimney is somewhat noticeable 75 feet up. Preying Mantle is a short route beginning just before the cliff enters the main quarry.

Descent from the Main Wall and Narrow Arrow areas is best accomplished via rappels, although hardy bushwhackers can outflank everything by traveling left from the wall's summit. From the Breakfast of Champions finish, hike over to the Slab's rappel route. Routes over to 10% MV can be descended in the same manner or rappelled by any number of routes. The best descent for routes ending on top of the wall, from Japanese Gardens to Free at Last, is via the City Park/Godzilla line. A rappel route from near the summit of the Narrow Arrow is in place down the Buried Treasure. One can also down climb and do short rappels down the Narrow Arrow route. With the exception of the Slab and Narrow Arrow route, all these descents require two ropes.

Orc Tower is the large pinnacle on the right side of the quarry. One can only speculate and grieve for the adventures that have been lost due to the turn-of-the-century quarrying. Some lines remain, but questionable rock has so far put off most investigations.

The climbs farthest right are in The Country and can be identified by the obvious white face cracks just before the cliff ends in the forest. The approach is via the tracks, then directly through the woods.

The Lower Lump is several hundred yards to the left of the Lower Wall. The Lowest Lump is the small "peak" separate from the main cliff.

MAIN WALL
E. Iron Horse   **N.** Narrow Arrow Overhang
L. City Park   **V.** Quarry Crack

THE SLAB

A. LEO CHIMNEY
I, 5.4; nuts to 2″

Either climb to the Railroad Bolts via the pitch below them or scramble up under the Black Wall. The chimney is often wet.

B. VELVASHEEN
I, 5.6; nuts to 3″

Use either approach mentioned in Leo Chimney, then climb cracks just right of the chimney. Join the Great Northern Route just below the top.

C. ARCHIES
I, 5.6; nuts to 2″

Follow obvious arches to the right of Velvasheen, passing through the upper pitch of the Great Northern Route under a roof, to a small fir tree.

D. THE GREAT NORTHERN ROUTE
I, 5.6; nuts to 3″

From the Railroad Bolts, reached by minimal fifth-class climbing, pass through an overhang to a ledge below a slab. Follow the left crack to the ring belay/rappel. Angle left under a roof and continue to the top.

E. PISCES
I, 5.10a; nuts to 2″

Follow the steep crack to the right of the Railroad Bolts to the slab, then climb the right-hand crack.

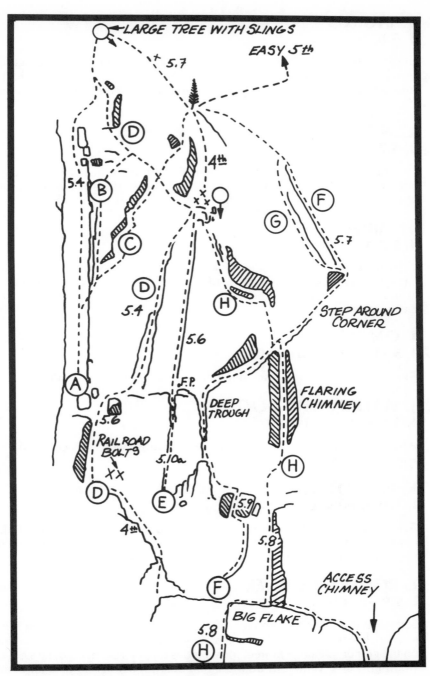

INDEX LOWER TOWN WALL: THE SLAB

F. TAURUS
I, 5.8; nuts to 2"

Begin at the Sickle-Blockbuster (the 5.9 can be avoided) and then climb a trough to the right of Pisces to a belay under the Aries roof. Angle right, then move through a small roof to the right of two parallel cracks. Belay at the small fir.

G. SWORDPLAY
I, 5.7; nuts to 1"

This moves through the small roof, then takes the left of the two parallel cracks mentioned in Taurus. Stay left of a small bush, belay at the fir, then continue to the top staying very close to a rib.

H. ARIES
I, 5.8; nuts to 3"

Start at ground level in a wide crack next to a large fir. From a ledge, continue up a left-facing corner, then up the black Aries Chimney to a large roof which is turned on its left side. The four short pitches of this route end at the ring belay/rappel.

I. ON THE VERGE
I, 5.11 +; fixed protection

This is the short face/layback immediately right of the Aries Chimney.

J. WALKIN' THE DOG
I, 5.10c, A0; nuts to ½"

An old bolt stud marks the beginning of this route. Higher, a second A0 move leads to a 5.10c crack.

K. NICKOTIME
I, 5.10a; nuts to 2"

Belay at the small roof where Taurus and Swordplay divide. Step right, then climb a left-trending arch into the trees above. The Slanting Crack variation steps across, then continues up a ramp to Roger's Corner.

L. ROGER'S CORNER
I, 5.9; nuts to 3"

Scramble up under the junction of the slab and the steep wall. Begin in a smooth, left-facing corner below a broken chimney. From the belay, continue up the corner to a large fir tree. Most parties rappel from here, but it's easy to worm upwards. Variation: from the first belay, move left to a small corner, then rejoin the route below a set of roofs.

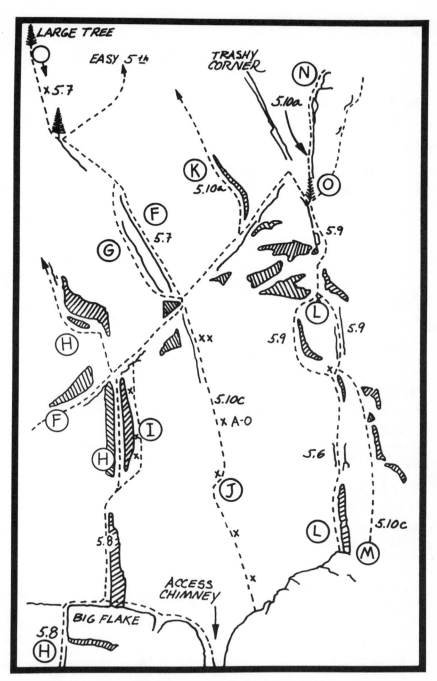

INDEX LOWER TOWN WALL: THE SLAB

M. SUGAR BEAR
I, 5.10c; nuts to 1"

This is the steep, blocky face just right of Roger's first pitch. Protection can be difficult to arrange.

N. BREAKFAST OF CHAMPIONS
I, 5.10a; nuts to 3"

From the large fir on Roger's, climb the left crack on the steep wall.

O. WINDMILLS
I, 5.11; nuts to 2"

From the large fir on Roger's, climb the right crack on the steep wall.

MAIN WALL

A. SNOW WHITE
II, 5.7, A3; 30 nuts and pins from RURPS to 1"

Start in a pin-scarred, thin crack on the left edge of the Main Wall. Climb up to an arch, reach left to a bolt, then nail up to a good ledge. Next, either traverse right under a roof or nut the right-hand crack system above the belay.

B. PRINCELY AMBITIONS
I, 5.8; nuts to 2"

Begin in obvious cracks immediately right of Snow White, go left of the large block on Frog Pond and climb the corner to the Snow White ledge. Finish the route up the left-hand crack system.

C. FROG POND
III, 5.9, A2; 30 nuts and pins, knifeblades to 2½"

Several hook moves lead to bolts beneath a roof. Traverse left to a belay at a small cedar. The second pitch moves up near a large block and then up to a ledge. A variation climbs cracks above, then right of the belay, and onto the ledge. The final pitch climbs a prominent corner to the Park Bench system.

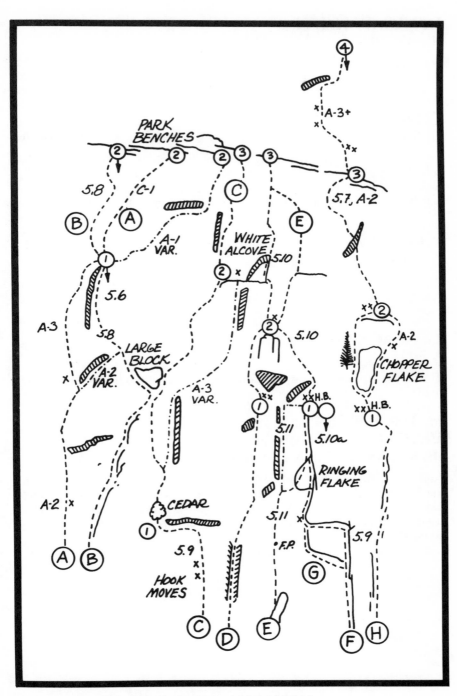

INDEX LOWER TOWN WALL: MAIN WALL

D. NUMBAH TEN
III, A3; 30 nuts and pins to 1"

Start in a "V-shaped" corner between Frog Pond and Iron Horse. Belay 100 ft. up under some overhangs. A short pitch passes through these roofs either right or left, ending on a good platform. One more pitch ends on the Park Bench.

E. IRON HORSE
II, 5.11, A1, or 5.7, A1; 30 nuts to 2½" with a few thin pitons

Free climbing or easy aid on nuts leads past many bolts and the Ringing Flake to a hanging belay under a roof. Turn the roof on the right and move up to a ledge. The third pitch ends on the Park Bench. Variation: climb the corner left of the Ringing Flake, then traverse over to the hanging belay, 5.11, or continue straight up over a roof, A2.

F. SAGITTARIUS
I, 5.10a; nuts to 3"

The climb traverses under a large roof past a bolt, passing the Ringing Flake on its right side. The climb finishes at the hanging belay mentioned on the Iron Horse route.

G. ARACHNID ARCH
I, 5.11

This is the arch below the Sagittarius belay. This climb has yet to receive a lead.

H. TEN PERCENT METEOROLOGICAL VINCULATION (10% MV)
III, 5.7, A3 +; 35 nuts and pins to 1½"

Nail face cracks to the right of Sagittarius to a hanging belay. A long pitch leads past the Chopper Flake via one of two cracks to a ledge under the Shield. Two difficult pitches lead up this blankish area. Many other belays could be used, for example the tree to the left of the Chopper, then the hanging belay some 45 ft. up the Shield.

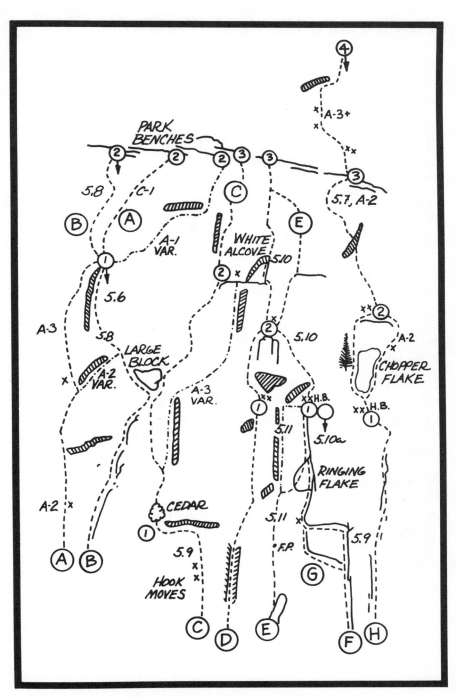

INDEX LOWER TOWN WALL: MAIN WALL

I. THROUGH THICK AND THIN (TT&T)
I, 5.11 +; nuts to 3"

Start at the lowest point of the rock, just right of 10% MV. Climb past a bolt to obvious wide flakes. From their end a thin crack leads to a tiny ledge. Rappel back down with two ropes.

J. JAPANESE GARDENS
III, 5.6, A2; 35 nuts and pins to 1½"

Use the same start as TT&T to the bolt, then move right to a dihedral system. Traverse left under a roof to the tiny ledge mentioned in TT&T. A variation is to belay under the roof, then turn it on the right. The second pitch of either variation ends on the Park Bench system. Next locate a corner with a prominent tree in it and follow the system to its immediate right. Another pitch climbs corners left of a large roof to a brushy ledge. Scrambling leads to the top.

K. ARTIFICE
III, 5.7, A2; 35 nuts and pins to 1½" (many small)

Just left of City Park is a small roof/alcove. Reach this via an arch system or from one-half way up City Park. A mixed pitch leads to the Park Bench. Easy aid up the system left of the City Park/Godzilla rappel leads to a small tree belay. One more mixed pitch leads to the top.

L. CITY PARK
I, C1; 30 nuts to 1" (mostly small)

This is the very obvious pin-scarred crack. The route starts with a bolt ladder, 5.10a if done free. This straight-in crack very readily takes nuts and leads to a comfortable ledge 120 ft. up.

M. GODZILLA
II, 5.10a; nuts from tiny to 3"

Godzilla is the major system right of City Park. The first long pitch ends on the City Park ledge. Next, free climb the old City Park second pitch past several bolts to the Park Bench. Most parties rappel from here, although it's possible to fight dirt to the top.

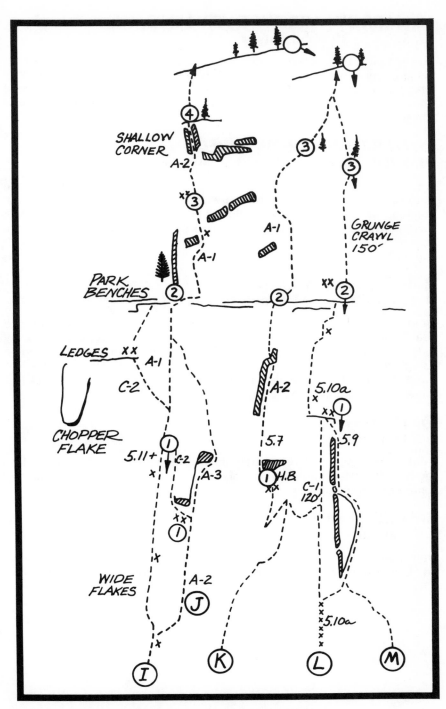

INDEX LOWER TOWN WALL: MAIN WALL

N. NARROW ARROW OVERHANG
III, 5.7, C3; 30 small nuts

The first pitch uses nuts and bolts, via one of two crack systems, to reach a hanging belay under the overhang. Tiny nuts take one over this obstacle, where mixed climbing leads to an enclosed belay ledge. Some parties rappel from here, while others continue free up and over the left side of the Narrow Arrow Pinnacle.

O. NARROW ARROW DIRECT
III, 5.10d, A2; nuts to 4" with a few pins for the aid section

A short free pitch leads to the Grey Snag. Aid then takes one to the ledge immediately right of the Narrow Arrow Overhang. An almost free method of reaching this ledge is to climb Buried Treasure's second pitch and then traverse over left. From the ledge, two crack pitches lead to a belay below the summit cleft. A short pitch leads to a ledge a few feet below the Arrow's summit.

P. BURIED TREASURE
II, 5.10b, C3, or 5.11 +; nuts to 3"

From the Grey Snag move right and climb an arch. From the arch's top, go straight up difficult free climbing or several points of aid below a rappel/belay ledge. The right-hand crack system leads up to a small roof which is turned on its right to the Park Bench system. A variation, Freedom Fighter, takes the left-hand crack to a ledge. The final pitch goes straight up past a shaky block to a varied crack, ending a few feet right of the Rotten Tree.

Q. THIN FINGERS
I, 5.11a; nuts to 2"

Climb the first pitch of Free at Last or traverse from the Buried Treasure arch to the base of a clean, white crack. From the crack's top, either rappel with two ropes or continue upward via one of several possibilities.

R. HARD AS HELL
I, 5.10b; nuts to 3"

From the tree-covered Park Bench, climb a crack left of the Dirty Dihedral to an obvious undercling; join Buried Treasure to the top.

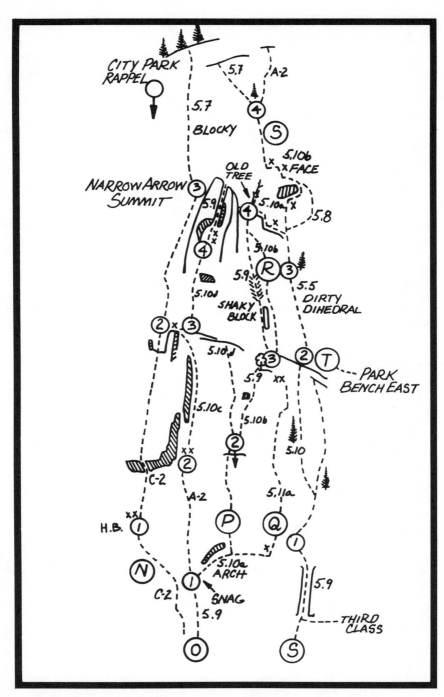

INDEX LOWER TOWN WALL: NARROW ARROW

S. FREE AT LAST
III, 5.10b; nuts to 3"

The first pitch climbs the shallow square chimney below and right of Thin Fingers. Approach the chimney via a ledge from the right or from directly below. Twenty feet after the belay ledge, choose one of two crack systems to the Park Bench. Garden up the Dirty Dihedral, pass a ledge to a clean left-facing corner and belay at a bolt. Next, turn the roof just above directly or take an easier line out to the right. Higher on the same pitch, face climb past two bolts to a belay from a small tree. One more short pitch leads to the top.

T. THE NARROW ARROW
II, 5.6; nuts to 3"

This has been worked out as the easiest way to reach the Narrow Arrow Pinnacle. Right of the Quarry Crack and shortly before the cliff turns into the main quarried wall, two 5.6 variations will lead to the extreme east end of the Park Bench system, 80 ft. above the ground. Move the belay over to a small fir at the base of the Dirty Dihedral. Climb this, mantle onto a ledge, then squeeze up to a chockstone belay. One more short, moderate pitch via one of several variations leads to a belay on the east side of the summit. Continuation: two 5.7 pitches start west of the notch and lead up via blocky climbing.

U. WITH APOLOGIES TO WALTER B.
I. 5.11; nuts to 1"

Uphill from Free at Last and left of the Quarry Crack is a small dihedral with a ledge at its base. Step over from the Quarry Crack route, use a bolt to protect a face move, then climb the dihedral.

V. QUARRY CRACK
I, 5.9; nuts to 3"

Start up blocky ledges to reach the wide crack which ends on the Park Bench East.

W. PREYING MANTLE
I, 5.10c; nuts to 1½"

Undercling, jam and climb an overhang for a short distance to reach a ledge just before the blocky area fades into the main quarry wall.

X. TAI AND RANDY MEMORIAL
I, 5.10d; nuts to 2"

From the extreme end of the Park Bench East, a short crack above will be obvious.

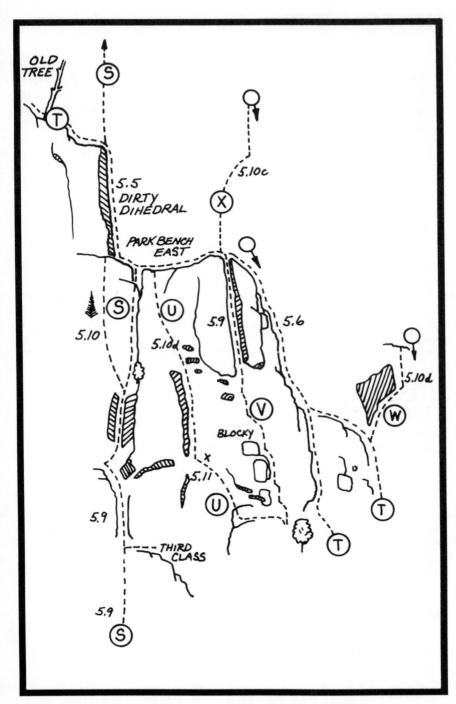

INDEX LOWER TOWN WALL: NARROW ARROW

THE COUNTRY

The climbs in The Country are usually approached by walking on the tracks right of the Lower Wall. A white crack, the third pitch of Heart of the Country, will be visible just before the rock disappears into the jungle. Hike directly to the base of the route. In the early season, this area may be swampy; if that is a problem, it is possible to hike under the wall from the Narrow Arrow area on the Main Wall.

A. HEART OF THE COUNTRY
II, 5.11b; nuts to 3"

From the left, reach a ledge 30 ft. above the ground. A large maple just right of a 20-ft. block provides the first belay. Climb the block, then angle right to the tree-covered ledge. This pitch requires a 5.9 or 5.10 move some 15 ft. from protection with serious fall consequences. From the ledge's left side, climb a crack which passes a large, jammed flake on its right side, then face climb over to a belay at the base of the white crack. From the crack's top, a short, overhanging, thin crack leads to the finish. Three single-rope rappels lead back down, although it is possible to hike off.

B. FOOL'S GOLD
I, 5.9; nuts to 2"

Climb the Country block, then face climb straight up to the left side of a gold wall. From the top of the gold-colored wall, traverse over to the tree ledge.

C. THE G-M ROUTE
II, 5.9; nuts to 3"

Walk across the first Country ledge to a bolt. Climb cracks up to the right edge of the tree ledge. From the back edge of this bench, go up past steep flakes and cracks to the end of the Country's second pitch. Next, move left up a wide crack, then step back out onto the main wall. Follow this system to the finish.

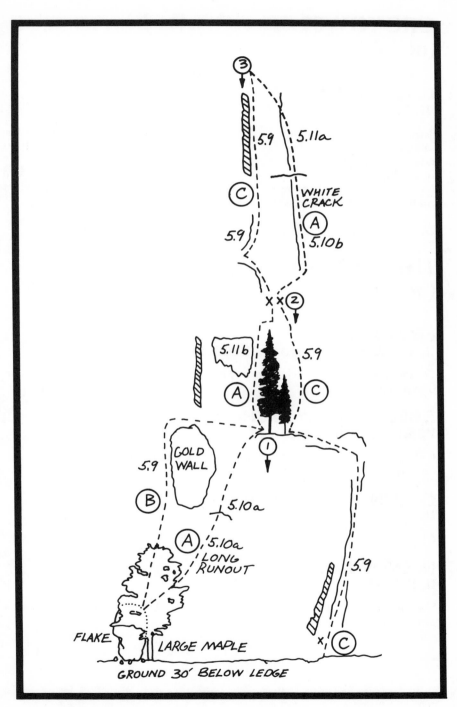

THE COUNTRY

ORC TOWER
(not shown)

D. ORC TOWER
III, 5.7, A3

This is the obvious pinnacle on the right edge of the quarry. Begin below the left edge of the tower and climb free, 5.7, to a fir, then nail a crack to a tree-covered ledge. Free up and right on ledges to a large deciduous tree at the base of a dihedral. Aid in the corner, then free up a chimney and lead to a ledge at the base of the tower. The final pitch aids a prominent crack system on the south wall to a free ramp and chimney.

THE LOWER LUMP
(not shown)

E. CONFETTI
II, 5.7, A2; 25 pins from a RURP to a 2″ angle

On the left side of the arch, climb two pitches free to where one can aid the overhangs.

F. BEETLE BAILEY ARCH
II, 5.8, A3; hardware to 2″

Follow a straight-in crack in the middle of the slab to where the overhangs can be climbed.

G. CONGOLINDINATION
II, 5.8, A3

Climb up and left to the right side of the arch and continue out to the right.

H. SNOWDONIA
II, 5.7, A1

Start at a lone 6-ft. pine tree on the far side of the Lump. The climb involves a ramp leading to a long gully.

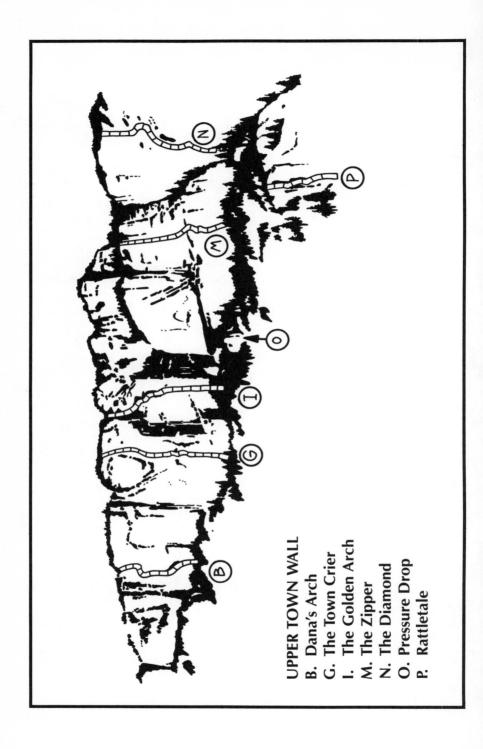

UPPER TOWN WALL
B. Dana's Arch
G. The Town Crier
I. The Golden Arch
M. The Zipper
N. The Diamond
O. Pressure Drop
P. Rattletale

UPPER TOWN WALL

Upper Town Wall routes are quite easy to locate if a few minutes are spent studying them from town. The Golden Arch is perhaps the most striking feature of the wall. The Abraxas and The Ave routes take the wall to its right. The Zipper route on The Cheeks utilizes the Ice Cream Scoop, a huge roof 80 feet above the ground and below a huge ledge, the Prance Platform. This ledge can be reached by 5.6 climbing on the Perverse Traverse. The Cheeks lie above the Prance Platform. The Diamond route lies off to the right of a creek or gully. Back left of the arch, one sees a huge, dirty chimney and gully system about a hundred yards away. The Davis-Holland route finishes up the top of this system, but the majority of the climbs, as well as the closely aligned Green Drag-On and Town Crier routes, are approximately halfway between this feature and the arch. Lamplighter is the next major system to the left. It is followed by Dana's Arch, the first pitch of which is not visible from town but is easily located from the base.

UPPER TOWN WALL

A. THE BACK ROAD (not shown)
II, 5.8; nuts to 2″

About 300 ft. left of Lamplighter, a boulder problem leads to a ledge with a small bush. Climb, 5.7, past a flake to a large ledge; move over left to a dihedral, then face climb right to a ledge and a crack system. The third pitch belays at the top of the cracks under an overhang. Continue above the roof up a mossy gully and chimney system.

B. DANA'S ARCH
III, 5.8, A3; 35 nuts and pins to 2½″

Begin in the obvious arch left of Lamplighter. Climb up the arch, then up to Cheeto Ledge. Move straight up past a flake, then over left to a belay ledge. Two more pitches involving 5.8 face climbing and a short section of nailing lead to scrambling and the top.

C. LAMPLIGHTER
IV, 5.8, A3; 30 nuts and pins to 2½″

Five pitches, mostly free with short sections of aid, lead up an obvious line.

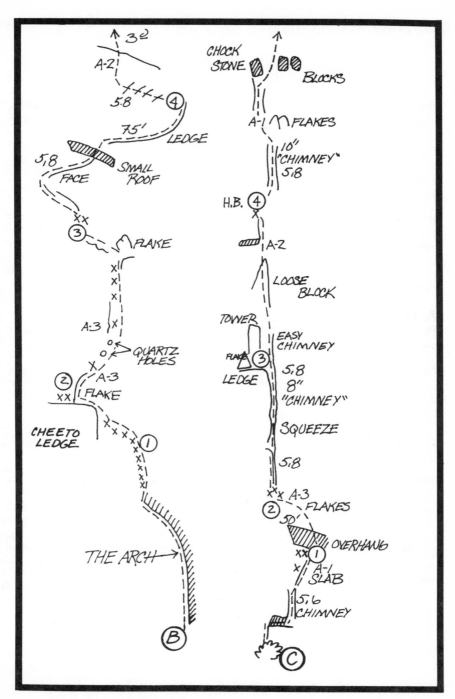

INDEX UPPER TOWN WALL

D. DAVIS-HOLLAND
II, 5.10b; nuts to 3"

Step out on a ledge to a clean crack leading to the extensive ledge system shared by the Davis, Drag-On and Crier routes. The second pitch follows the large, left-facing corner to a semi-hanging belay under a roof. Turn this roof, then climb to a good ledge. It is now possible to rappel via two 150 footers or to continue up. To continue, whack left on ledges to the base of a chimney and gully system; tread lightly to the top. The decision of whether or not to climb the upper section is usually based on where the car is parked.

E. LOVIN' ARMS
III, 5.10b, A0; nuts to 3"

Begin with the first three pitches of the Davis-Holland route. From the ledge three pitches up, climb the right of several cracks into the wide chimney which is followed 40' to a semi-hanging belay. Next, move out right onto the face, use one A0 move from a bolt, then continue upwards to a ledge. The final pitch face climbs directly above the belay, finishing midway between the two pines on top.

F. THE GREEN DRAG-ON
IV, 5.4, A3; 40 nuts and pins from knifeblades to 3", including 15 Lost Arrows and blades plus hooks

Nail cracks 25 ft. to the right of Davis-Holland's first pitch to the ledges. Continue up a right-facing corner to a hanging belay. The third belay is under a roof which is turned on the right. Strenuous aid and hook moves lead to a belay from a bolt ladder. Easy nailing and free climbing lead to the top.

G. THE TOWN CRIER
IV, 5.8, A2; nuts plus 20 pins, including 5 Lost Arrows to 3"

Either free climb the first pitch of the Davis or nail the first Drag-On pitch to the ledge system. If aid is used on the first Davis pitch, please use nuts only, for pitons are destroying this beautiful crack. The second pitch proceeds free up a chimney to a comfortable belay beneath Big Honker Ledge. Move up a short arch to a small belay ledge, then travel through the Triple Overhangs to a hanging belay. Bolts and wide cracks lead to another hanger at the base of a long bolt ladder. Climb this ladder, then traverse onto broken ground. A short free pitch leads to the top.

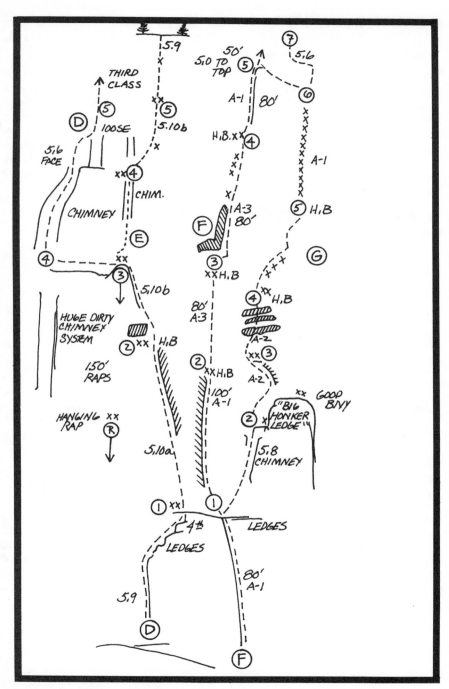

INDEX UPPER TOWN WALL

H. WATERWAY LEFT
**IV, 5.7, A3; 40 nuts and pins from 5 knifeblades to two 2"
angles; many Lost Arrows**

This route is intimately tied with the waterfall and therefore should be attempted only when it is relatively dry. Right of the Davis route is a long roof a short distance above the ground. A third-class ledge leads out to where the roof is turned near its right edge. Aid then leads out to the left side of a discontinuous ledge. Move to the right of this ledge, then climb up to a roomy one. Next, continue up, pendulum left, then continue up to a hanging belay. Two more pitches with some mandatory free climbing lead across the waterfall to join The Golden Arch. The final pitch, a chimney, can be difficult when wet.

I. THE GOLDEN ARCH
IV, 5.7, A3 +; 40 nuts and pins from knifeblades to 2½"

Start on a big flake to the right of the waterfall. An aid pitch leads to a ledge with a tree. A short free pitch leads up to Madsen's Ledge at the base of the Golden Arch. Two pitches up the Arch, using hooks and nuts to save delicate flakes on the upper section, lead to a ledge belay. Two more short pitches lead to the top.

J. ABRAXAS
IV, 5.7, A3; 40 nuts and pins from RURPS to 3"

Two pitches left of the Arch start, the first beginning at a flake and ending on a ledge with a small tree, end on Madsen's Ledge. Shift the belay past the Arch, then aid several complicated pitches through roofs and past flakes and hook moves. After an exposed hanging belay above a roof, move over, then join The Ave to the top. This route is currently the wall's most consistently difficult.

K. THE AVE
**IV, 5.8, A4; 40 nuts and pins from RURPS to 3" (heavy on the
Lost Arrows and small angles)**

Right of The Golden Arch's first pitch, a 150-ft chimney/crack system leads from the ground to Madsen's Ledge. After moving the belay right, nail diagonally along a roof to a hanging belay. Continue along, then turn up to another hanging belay. A long pitch leads to a semi-hanging belay, followed by awkward nailing to a tree. Third-class moves exit off to the top.

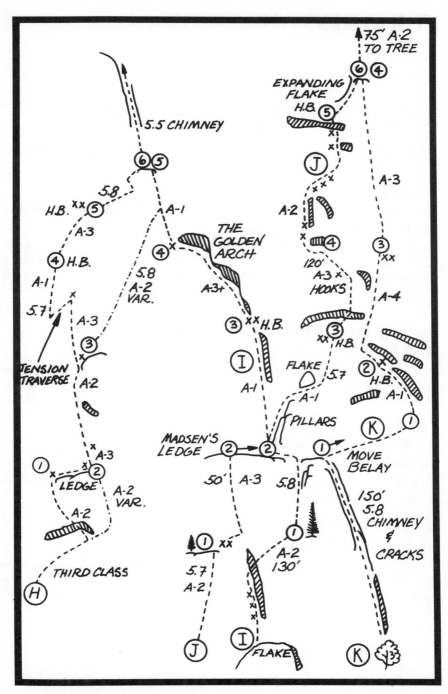

INDEX UPPER TOWN WALL

THE CHEEKS AND DIAMOND

L. WILMON'S WALKABOUT (not shown)
III, 5.5, A3

Mixed climbing on the extreme left edge of The Cheeks starts just before the Perverse Traverse.

M. THE ZIPPER
IV, 5.10b, A2; 40 nuts and pins from 5 knifeblades to 4" (many small nuts for the first pitch)

Start below the Ice Cream Scoop and climb to a hanging belay just below it, 5.10b. A2 aid through the roof is followed by a short pitch to the Prance Platform. A mixed free and aid pitch then leads to the base of an open book which is followed to the top. Descend by walking and rappelling down and left.

N. THE DIAMOND (DIHEDRAL ROUTE)
IV, 5.8, A4; 50 nuts and pins, mostly under 1", to 2½"

Traverse over from the base of The Zipper to the obvious corner. Either travel out a ledge to the start or start down lower and tunnel up behind a giant block. Aid leads up the corner to the top of The Diamond, where two more free pitches travel to the summit. Descend by walking and rappelling right.

O. PRESSURE DROP
I, 5.11b; nuts to 1"

Branch off the main trail, heading toward The Zipper, just below the Main Wall. Pressure Drop lies on a boulder just past the junction.

P. RATTLETALE
II, 5.10a; nuts to 3"

The route lies on the left-hand side of a white wall as seen from town and on the overview drawing. The climb consists of three crack pitches: 5.6, 5.10a and 5.8.

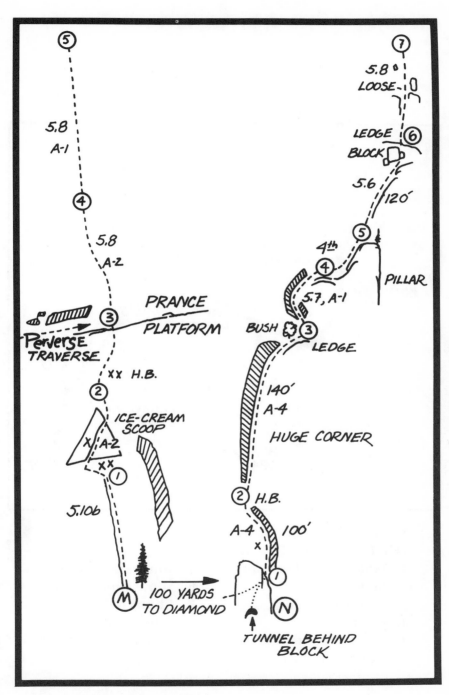

INDEX UPPER TOWN WALL

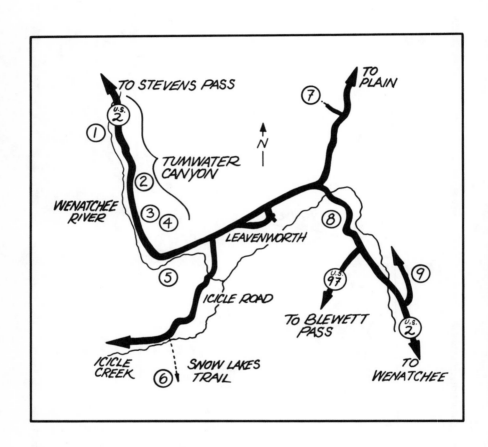

THE LEAVENWORTH AREA

1. **Waterfall Column and Jupiter Rock**
2. **Rattlesnake Rock**
3. **Castle Rock**
4. **Midnight and Noontime Rocks**
5. **Tumwater Tower**
6. **Snow Creek Wall**
7. **Chumstick Snag**
8. **Sandy Slab**
9. **Peshastin Pinnacles**

LEAVENWORTH

Leavenworth is both a small town in central Washington and the comprehensive name given to numerous cliffs forming Washington's major rock-climbing center. Located on the east side of the Cascade Mountains, the area is approached via U.S. Highway 2 from the east or west or from Highway 97 to the south. All services from food and gas to a small hospital are available in the decorative Bavarian village of Leavenworth. Overnight camps are usually made somewhere in the Icicle Canyon.

Unusual dangers inherent in Leavenworth climbing include ticks in the spring and summer, rattlesnakes in the hot months, the opening of hunting season in the fall and the Autumn Leaf and Mai Fest celebrations.

While Tumwater Canyon, Icicle Canyon and Peshastin Pinnacles are all Leavenworth rock-climbing areas, they differ enough to be treated separately. Tumwater Canyon begins immediately on the western end of the town of Leavenworth. The Icicle Road turnoff is also located in this same vicinity. The Snow Lakes Trail parking lot will be some four miles up this road. On the eastern end of town, the Plain Canyon Road leads to the small Chumstick Snag. By continuing east on U.S. 2 from town, one will reach the other sandstone areas. Sandy Slab, immediately along the road, is about 2½ miles out. In another seven miles the Peshastin Pinnacles will come into view on the left. Another few miles takes one into the town of Wenatchee.

TUMWATER CANYON

Nestled deep in Tumwater Canyon, three miles west of the town of Leavenworth, is Castle Rock. Higher up the hill, commanding a greater view of the raging Wenatchee River, Drury Falls and the Icicle Ridge, is Midnight Rock. These two small cliffs contain an awesome concentration of routes, probably as great as any granite crags in the country. Midnight Rock, approximately 150 feet high and 300 feet wide, contains 40 pitches, mostly difficult cracks. Castle Rock has an even greater concentration with more variety; cracks, faces and roofs predominate here. Several lesser-known and less frequently climbed cliffs are scattered about the canyon, as well; but most of the action takes place on Castle and Midnight.

Logger's Ledge divides Castle Rock into an upper and lower section. This feature was named when certain people, most active here in the fifties and sixties, removed "offending vegetation," some of it reaching a foot or two in diameter! People walking on this ledge must be aware of the climbers below and so tread carefully on loose rocks. Lower Castle is an athletic area, abounding in roofs, some skirted and others attacked directly. Upper Castle sports more variety with routes of all fifth-class difficulties, from the moderate Sabre to a number of 5.11 routes.

Several years ago when Castle Rock listed some 30 routes, certain people were overheard to declare it "climbed out." It now has around 50 routes, and while few major, multi-pitch lines remain, a tremendous number of short, extreme problems exist.

Named for an epic rescue on its first ascent, Midnight Rock is reached by an ever-deteriorating trail from Castle's summit. More than any other area in this guidebook, Midnight Rock deserves to be described as an expert's area. The easiest climb, a strenuous 5.8 + route, leaves little room for error. The hardest routes will rarely even be tried, especially by those who have seen them! Relatively few take the somewhat arduous hike up the hill, but those who do, provided their level of fitness and technique is fairly high, will be vastly rewarded.

Waterfall Column and Jupiter Rock are two other areas in this canyon; climbing on them is an adventure quite different from others in this book. The difficult approach results in few people and a reduced potential for rescue assistance. Routes are also difficult to locate and follow due to the discontinuous nature of the walls. On the positive side there is a freedom, away from the crowds, that a person who climbs only on Castle Rock will never understand.

There are other cliffs in the Tumwater. Rattlesnake, Piton Tower and Tumwater Tower have been climbed on for over 30 years but deserve more attention. Other well-known but unpublicized cliffs and a large number of relatively undiscovered rocks will also draw those wishing to escape the harsh glare of the Castle and Midnight scenes. Adequate room for all is still available in this magical canyon.

CASTLE ROCK

The Upper Castle Rock trail begins on the north side of the parking lot. It reaches the rock near Lower Rainshadow and continues along Logger's Ledge under all the Upper Castle Rock routes. The Lower Castle Rock trail leaves the lot from the south side. It first comes to the Lower Rock with the fault chimney and its neighbors. Third classing on the left side leads above the steep, lower routes to give access to the roof routes. It is, of course, possible to start at the bottom and do one Lower Rock route (ending at Logger's Ledge), then one Upper Rock route, ending up on the summit where a trail leads back down.

UPPER CASTLE ROCK

A. THE NORTH RIDGE (not shown)
I, 5.5

This is the skyline, distinguished by a large pine halfway up.

B. LOWER RAINSHADOW
I, 5.11 +

This route is identified by two small trees on the left edge of a multicolored wall.

C. RAINBOW CONNECTION
I, 5.11a; nuts to 1″

Start from a large flake. Face climb past a thin crack to a roof; cross it, then take a shallow corner up to join Saints.

D. BY THE SEA
I, 5.10c; nuts to 2½″

Left of the Saints corner, two cracks run horizontally left. Follow these; surmount the roof (the same one as on route C), then traverse back right to the Angel ledge.

E. SAINTS-RAINSHADOW
II, 5.9; nuts to 2″

Follow Saints to the tree, then climb up to and around a large roof. Flakes and face climbing lead to the top.

F. SAINTS
II, 5.8; nuts to 2″

Begin in a 15-ft. flaring corner and work up and left to a tree. Angle right, then up a rib/face to the top.

G. SHORT AND SASSY
I, 5.9 +; nuts to 1″

Move right after the Saints corner.

H. ANGEL
II, 5.7; nuts to 2"

Climb up the greasy Angel Crack (5.10, usually bouldered) to a large ledge. Move left, then up a long pitch to a belay ledge to the right of a shaky block. Variation: a corner leads off the right side of the big ledge to pass right of a smooth section. Join the regular route (minimal protection). Easier rock on either variation leads to the top in one more pitch.

I. DAMNATION
I, 5.9; nuts to 3"

This is the obvious crack on the long side of Jello Tower.

J. UPPER DAN'S DREADFUL DIRECT
I, 5.9; nuts to 1"

Start via the Angel variation (5.10) or from high up Damnation. Continue up the relatively featureless face.

K. M.F. OVERHANG
I, 5.10c; nuts to 1"

This route is on the corner of the north and river faces of Jello Tower.

L. MIDWAY DIRECT
I, 5.6; nuts to 1"

Step off Jello Tower and continue straight up. A variation, Heavenly Traverse, goes left and joins Angel.

M. WINTER SOLSTICE
I, 5.6; nuts to 2"

Skirt the roof to the right of Jello Tower to a belay below the chimney. Two more pitches right of the chimney lead to the top.

N. DEVIL'S FRIGHT
I, 5.10b; nuts to 1½"

This route leads through the roof mentioned in route M.

O. THE NOSE
I, 5.10d; nuts to 1½"

This is on the river face of Jello Tower. Exiting below the crux makes the route 5.10c.

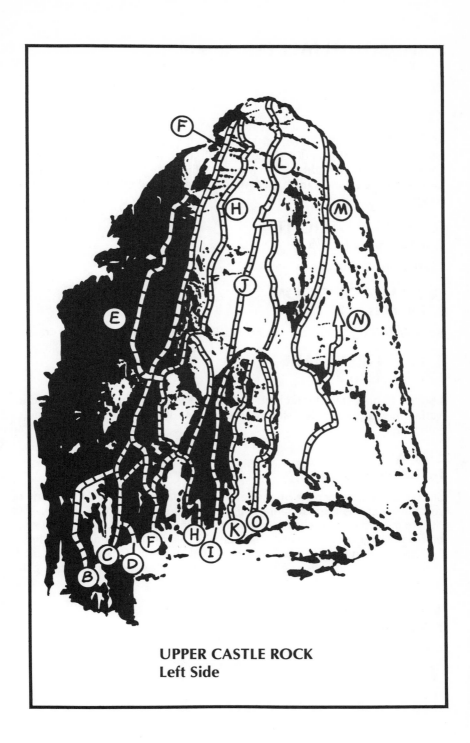

UPPER CASTLE ROCK
Left Side

P. THE SOUTH FACE (not shown)
I, 5.8; nuts to 2½"

This follows the crack system left of Midway Chimney past a bolt.

Q. MIDWAY
I, 5.5; nuts to 3"

Start on the uphill side of Jello Tower with a 5.5 first pitch. Step over to the main wall; traverse right into a chimney which is followed to a belay ledge (watch for rope drag). Finish the chimney, then follow cracks and face holds to the top.

R. DEVIL'S DELIGHT
I, 5.10c, nuts to 2½"

Go directly up a bubbly white wall.

S. CRACK OF DOOM
I, 5.9; nuts to 2"

Scramble up to a "sentry box" right of the white wall and climb a steep crack.

T. OLD GREY MARE
I, 5.7; nuts to 2"

Use the Canary start, then climb a prow just left of the prominent dihedral. Variation (Chicken Little): stay well to the left of the prow, 5.6. Both routes join S or U.

U. CANARY
II, 5.8; nuts to 2"

Start in a small corner down and left of the prominent dihedral. Use one of several variations to gain Sabre Ledge, 5.7. Variation (Canary Direct): start right of the first corner; climb the prominent dihedral, then exit to Sabre Ledge below the large roof, 5.8. Next, make an airy step off the left edge of the ledge and pass several bolts to a belay in a small alcove, 5.8. One more easy pitch leads to the top. Variation: after the two bolts, follow a line overlooking the Sabre Chimney, 5.7.

V. CAT BURGLAR
I. 5.6; nuts to 2"

From 20 ft. right of Canary, make a bouldering move onto a prominent ramp. Follow this around the corner to Sabre Ledge in one or two pitches. Variation: use a higher ramp to turn the corner, 5.9 +. Continue above the ledge along a line to the right of the Sabre Chimney to the top.

UPPER AND LOWER CASTLE ROCK

W. HANGDOG
I, 5.11a; nuts to 2"

From the start of the Cat Burglar ramp, go straight up, then under a small roof to a thin crack.

X. DIRETISSIMA
I, 5.8; nuts to 1"

Around the corner pass several caves, then locate an undercut corner. Climb this corner, then continue up the smooth wall left of the Sabre Dihedral to the ledge. Variation: a 5.9 start to the left leads to the base of the smooth wall. Move right off Sabre Ledge to locate another pitch to the top.

Y. SABRE
I, 5.4; nuts to 3"

Start up a small pedestal leading to the very prominent dihedral. From a belay on Sabre Ledge, continue up the chimney/corner to the top.

Z. ORANGE PEEL (not shown)
I, 5.9; nuts to 1"

Climb the left wall of the Sabre Chimney.

AA. CENTURY
I, 5.8; nuts to 2½"

Follow a rib to the right of the Sabre Dihedral to a belay beneath a roof. Skirt the roof on the left, pass a tree and continue upwards.

BB. ROOFER
I, 5.9; nuts to 2"

Follow a slab over small roofs to join the Century belay below the roof. Continue directly over the roof, then join Century to the top.

UPPER CASTLE ROCK
Far Right Side

LOWER CASTLE ROCK

a. CLEM'S LAYBACK
I, 5.8

On the left edge of the lower rock, several large roofs will be seen. Clem's takes a line just left of these.

b. MONKEY LIP
I, 5.11d

Monkey Lip follows a line directly through the roofs. Belay above the first, then climb another pitch, 5.11a, over the second roof.

c. APESVILLE
I, 5.11 +

Take a line left of Monkey Lip through the first roof, then traverse right under the second until it's possible to go up.

d. BRASS BALLS
I, 5.10a; nuts to 2″

Brass Balls also passes through overhangs, but they are smaller than those of the routes on either side of it. Begin in an alcove/roof 20 ft. above the third-class ramp; pass on the left edge of a white wall to more roofs, then up a left-facing corner.

e. SHRIEK OF THE MUTILATED
I, 5.12

Left of Catapult, several horizontal roofs with a thin crack through the first will be seen. Belay above the second roof, then climb a 5.10a pitch up and left to easy ground.

f. CATAPULT
I, 5.8; nuts to 2″

The major break through the area, this route lies above the chimney on the Fault route.

g. VERTEBRAE
I, 5.10b; nuts to 3″

Climb Catapult until it's possible to step right to Stone Ledge. Climb a crack to the left of The Spike, a protruding piece of rock.

h. THE BONE (PENSTEMON)
I, 5.9; nuts to 2″

From the third-class ramp, a 5.7 pitch leads to the right side of Stone Ledge. Another crack, this one passing The Spike on the right, leads to easy scrambling.

i. GORE ROOF
I, 5.10b; nuts to 2″

To the right of The Bone near a small tree, face and crack climbing lead through a roof.

j. J.J. OVERHANG
I, 5.10d

Follow the ramp right above The Boot, a large flake. J.J. is the route left of the Spectator Overhang.

k. SPECTATOR OVERHANG
I, 5.4, A0

Several fixed pins lead through a rotten roof.

l. GORILLA DESPERADO
I, 5.10a, A0

Use Spectator's fixed pins to protect a line just right.

m. IDIOT'S DELIGHT
I, 5.9; nuts to 3″

Right of the Spectator's area, another roof, this one slightly higher, is turned on its left side where several variations lead upwards.

n. BIRD'S NEST OVERHANG
I, 5.8 +; nuts to 2″

Either traverse under The Boot or enter from the right to the base of a white, right-facing corner. A 5.7 pitch leads to the right edge of the ramp and the overhang.

o. MR. CLEAN
I, 5.10c; nuts to 1″

Follow obvious thin, shallow cracks lying left of The Fault.

p. SMUT
I, 5.10a; small nuts

Smut lies between The Fault and Mr. Clean.

q. THE FAULT
I, 5.6; nuts to 3″

A pitch up the obvious chimney leads to a ledge under Catapult. Angle off right, staying under the roofs for one or two pitches.

r. CLEAN LOVE
I, 5.10b; nuts to 1″

Start up the right side of a pedestal.

s. AMY CARTER
I, 5.9

Move up an obvious arch on the right side of the rock.

t. FLYING FROG
I, 5.9+

Move up shallow cracks on a ramp.

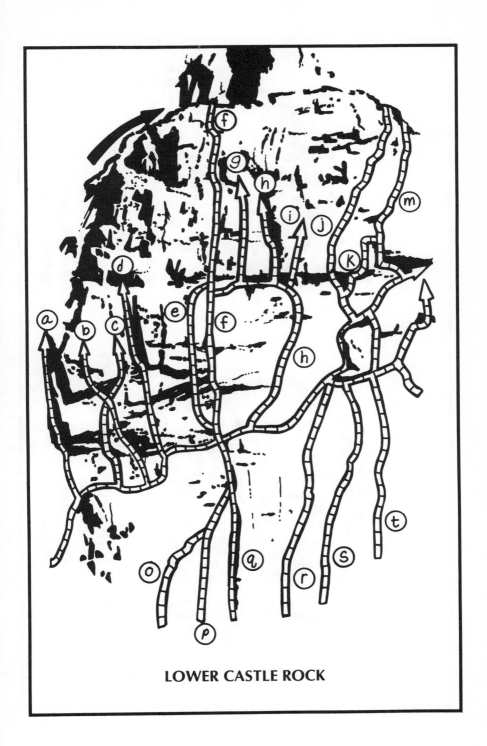

LOWER CASTLE ROCK

MIDNIGHT AND NOONTIME ROCKS

M. The Wild Traverse
W. Midnight Madness
X. South Ramp

Y. Shootout at High Noon
Z. Gulliver's Travels
AA. Wall Street

VOLKSWAGON LEDGE

DEAD END LEDGE

MIDNIGHT and NOONTIME ROCKS

Midnight and Noontime Rocks, sites of the most concentrated set of cracks in Washington State, are approached via a trail from the summit of Castle Rock. Dead End Ledge provides the access for most of the Midnight routes. The few exceptions include Curtains (above the Corner Crack on what could be termed the North Face), Spellbound (on the equally small South Face, approached from above or below), and Midnight Rambler, Midnight Madness, South Ramp and Super-crack (all reached from a scratch trail which leaves the main trail in view of the climbs). Noontime is also approached via this trail, which may be difficult to locate. The Midnight descent is down a simple trail on the north side of the rock. One look at the line drawings makes it obvious that many combinations of routes are possible given fitness, time, imagination and experience. Because climbs follow obvious lines, little or no descriptions are given for the routes that follow.

MIDNIGHT ROCK

A. CORNER CRACK
I, 5.9; nuts to 2"

This is a short crack above the Dead End Ledge Trail.

B. CURTAINS
I, 5.10d

Climb the flakes of the North Face; end on North Ramp.

C. NORTH RAMP
I, 5.10a; nuts to 2"

D. NIGHTINGALE
I, 5.10; nuts to 2"

E. YELLOWBIRD
I, 5.9; nuts to 1½"

The variation is 5.9.

F. SOMETIMES A GREAT NOTION
I, 5.10d

G. BLACK WIDOW
I, 5.10; nuts to 3"

H. EASTER OVERHANG
I, 5.9 +; nuts to 3"

I. TWIN CRACKS
I. 5.10b; nuts to 5"

J. R.O.T.C. (RATHER OVERHANGING THIN CRACK)
I, 5.11c

K. ROLLER COASTER CHIMNEY
I, 5.7; nuts to 1½"

Direct finish, 5.9.

L. J.A.M. SESSION (Jay, Al and Mead)
I, 5.10c; small nuts

Very few jams.

M. THE WILD TRAVERSE
I, 5.9; nuts to 1½"

N. SPELLBOUND
I, 5.11a

This route is on the South Face and joins The Wild Traverse.

O. IN SEARCH OF THE PERFECT PUMP
I, 5.11d/5.12

P. STING
I, 5.10b; nuts to 3"

Q. WASP
I, 5.10a; nuts to 3"

R. THE FLAME
I, 5.8 +; nuts to 3"

Direct start, 5.10a

S. FROG SUICIDE
I, 5.10a

T. DIAMOND IN THE ROUGH
I, 5.11a

U. SUPERCRACK
I, 5.11d/5.12; nuts to 4"

This is approached from the South Ramp.

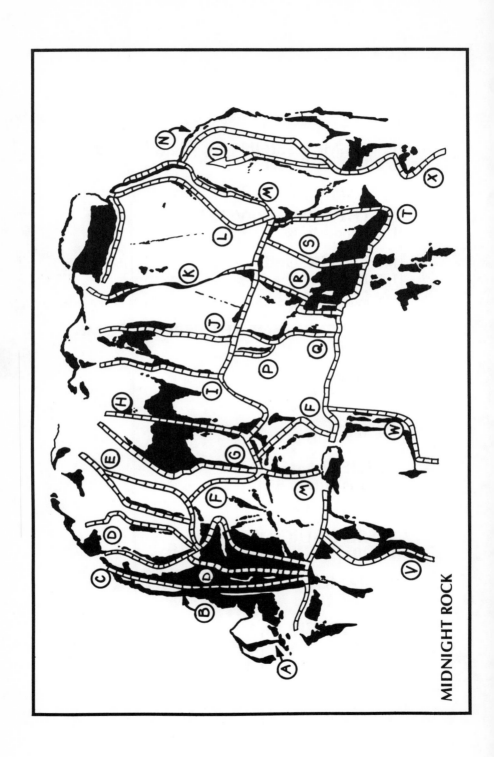

MIDNIGHT ROCK

V. MIDNIGHT RAMBLER
I, 5.7; nuts to 4"

This is a deep chimney.

W. MIDNIGHT MADNESS
I, 5.8 +; nuts to 3"

The second pitch traverses under a greenish roof.

X. SOUTH RAMP
II, 5.10a; nuts to 2"

NOONTIME ROCK

Y. SHOOTOUT AT HIGH NOON
I, 5.11a; nuts to 2"

Rappel from a tree to an apron, then start at a leaning flake.

Z. GULLIVER'S TRAVELS
I, 5.8, A1; hardware to 3"

AA. WALL STREET
I, 5.11, A3; hardware to 3"

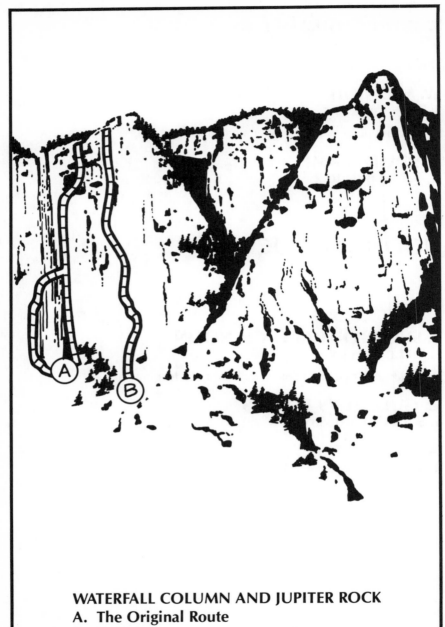

WATERFALL COLUMN AND JUPITER ROCK
A. The Original Route
B. Endgame

WATERFALL COLUMN
and JUPITER ROCK

Waterfall Column and Jupiter Rock share a strenuous approach. It parallels Drury Creek via ribs and gullies. The best approach, across the Wenatchee River, is by boat or wading (depending on the water level). Study crossings carefully as some potential crossings have serious consequences if a fall occurs. Plan on several hours to reach the start of technical climbing. It is also possible to begin at the Tumwater Campground, but this adds a fair distance to the walk.

Two descents from the top of the Waterfall routes are used: the first is to rappel the original route, the second climbs down a gully behind the buttress, then down a rib to Jupiter Rock. Expect at least two rappels and some fifth-class down climbing.

Like Waterfall Column, Jupiter Rock requires a complicated and touchy descent. Gullies on either side of the rock have been descended; both rappels and fifth-class down climbing are possible, therefore it is best to be prepared for the possibility of having to leave equipment behind.

A team would have to be extremely familiar with the approach and descents to do one of these routes in a day from the car, so it is best to plan on two or three days to get the feel of this place. The topos give only general outlines as to the possibilities on these walls. Because numerous variations and lines exist, it is best to be flexible and expect the unexpected.

WATERFALL COLUMN

A. THE ORIGINAL ROUTE
III, 5.8

The first-ascent party crossed the lower falls at their base, then back over at their top to begin climbing. Four pitches of chimneys and cracks lead to the top. A direct start of three pitches has been discovered, eliminating the need to cross the falls.

B. ENDGAME
IV, 5.9

A distance to the right of the falls is a Logger's Ledge-type terrace distinguished by a 7-ft roof. Start left of this undercut and follow cracks and ramps to a big ledge. Move two pitches and 10 ft. of a third lead to an unprotected, 5.2 traverse. The belay is either from some rock horns or a bit farther down on a ledge. The next belay is in a crack just down and left of a small tree. One more pitch leads to the top.

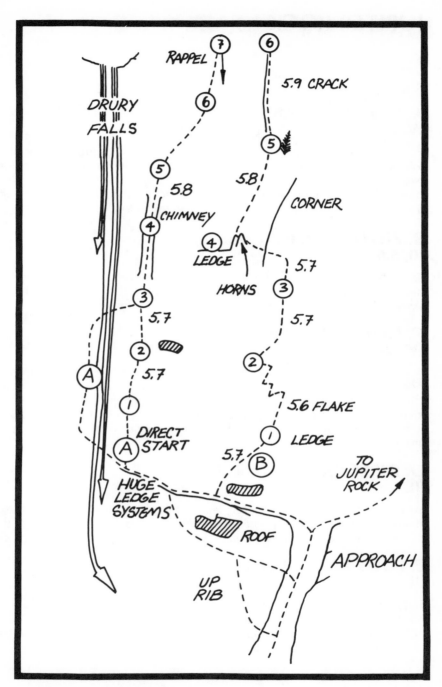

WATERFALL COLUMN

JUPITER ROCK

A. KING'S INDIAN
IV, 5.8

Begin approximately 70 yds. left of the lowest point of Jupiter Rock, then follow a major ramp and dihedral system to a large roof, obvious from below. Next move up and over to a minor ridge leading to a huge ledge with a prominent tree. Off this ledge, climb a right-facing dihedral to the right of the tree. Thread a tunnel and join Nimzo Indian to the top.

B. ZIGZAG (partially shown)
III, 5.6

From the toe of the rock, traverse left on a long ledge system for several hundred feet past a tree. At the end of the ledge, climb a ridge on the left skyline. Follow the ridge to the top via the crest for five leads.

C. NIMZO INDIAN
IV, 5.8

Begin at the lowest point of the buttress and proceed up to a pine tree. Continue up; go left to two small trees, then up to a ledge. After down climbing 15 ft., move past a flake to a block. A slot then leads to the ledges, giving access to a huge ledge with a big pine. Climb to a bushy tree, then follow a ramp to its end. Go up and around a corner to another tree and easier ground.

D. DIRECT ROUTE (not shown)
III, 5.6

Several hundred feet of scrambling lead to this climb, found to the right of a steep white wall. Climb up to a ledge right of an obvious chimney. Use the chimney and cracks to its left to gain the summit.

E. FOUR KNIGHTS (not shown)
III, 5.7

Follow Direct Route until a 5.0 traverse leads right to a large tree. Angle up and right to a small tree with a fair amount of foliage where a belay is set. Next, belay above a flake, then at a big ledge with another tree. One more fifth-class pitch leads to fourth-class steps and the finish.

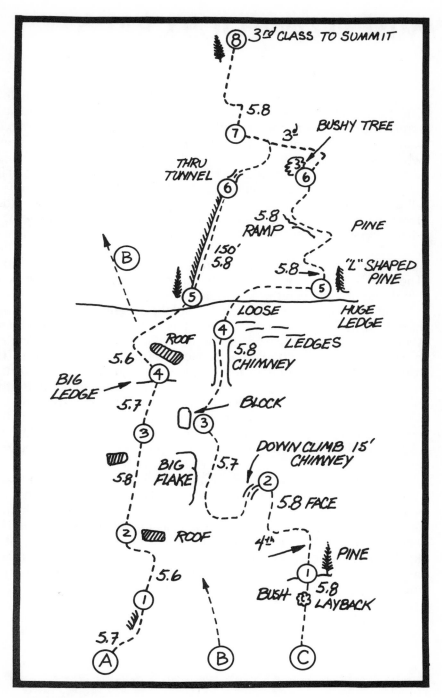

JUPITER ROCK

125

MISCELLANEOUS CRAGS

Eight-tenths of a mile up river from Castle Rock and approximately 600 feet above the road lie Rattlesnake Rock and Piton Tower. Park at a turnout, cross the road, and take the trail up to the lower right corner of Rattlesnake. Descent from Piton Tower involves a short rappel, whereas Rattlesnake is easy to walk off of.

Piton Tower is a rectangular block with a route running up each of its four faces. The East Face Notch route is 5.9 + or 5.10a, while the others all require some tricky aid. The Rattlesnake routes on the right side, The Viper Crack and The Shaky Pine, are obvious and distinctive. The Shaky Pine, 5.8, nuts to 2", leads up a corner under the multicolored wall. Begin with an easy crack and don't look for the shaky pine as it is gone. The Viper Crack, 5.7, nuts to 2", is just around the corner from The Shaky Pine route. A somewhat unprotected, 5.6 variation is to climb the rib between the two routes.

Over near the Piton-Rattlesnake notch, several more routes are found. Down from and east of the notch is a short, mossy chimney. The West Route climbs this chimney, then moves up under an overhanging block. Move right up past a ledge, then on up via easier ground. The route is 5.8 and requires a few small nuts. Immediately above the notch, a thin crack diagonals over to join The West Route under the block. This variation, The Whippet, is rated 5.8 when started via the face directly under the left extremity of the crack. Down and east of the notch is a huge boulder with a chimney on its left side. The Wildflower route uses this chimney, then continues up with some mixed free and aid.

Tumwater Tower is visible from several points on the hillside opposite the road near the Leavenworth end of the canyon. It is easiest to reach by crossing the bridge two miles west of town and then hiking along the river. All four routes require a normal nut selection. The Normal Route is 5.5 and begins on the inside corner. The Upper Notch Route is 5.6 and works out onto the north face. The southeast face involves 5.10 face climbing and 5.8 cracks. Finally, Highway Route on the north face is 5.8.

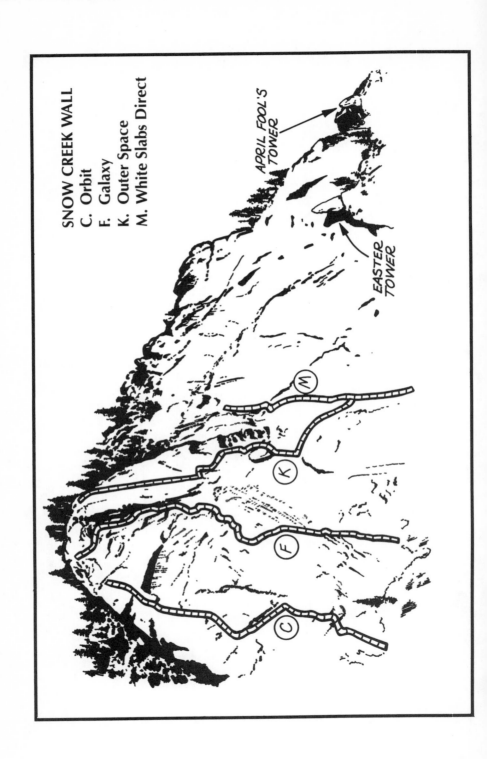

SNOW CREEK WALL
C. Orbit
F. Galaxy
K. Outer Space
M. White Slabs Direct

APRIL FOOL'S TOWER

EASTER TOWER

SNOW CREEK WALL

If the Tumwater is a magical canyon, then Icicle must be a place of mystery. Leavenworth's largest cliff, Snow Creek Wall, is located here and is fairly thoroughly documented, but routes on other walls are unrecorded. All along the Icicle Creek road the alert eye will spot problems ranging from ten feet to ten pitches. This guide, following tradition, is giving very little information about these climbs, preferring to let people stretch their legs and minds and discover for themselves what is hiding just up the hill. Perhaps the future holds a guide to these climbs; but for now, Icicle Canyon is still a place to escape crowds and to keep the pioneering spirit alive.

From the huge Snow Lakes Trail parking lot, an hour or so is required to approach the Snow Creek Wall. Seemingly endless switchbacks finally level out near the wall's right edge where several overviews of the climbs become possible. Below the Shield, a log crosses Snow Creek and provides access to campsites and the base trail.

The approach is justified by the tremendous concentration of long free routes. A majority of the climbs are in the five-pitch to seven-pitch range and are often at a standard that makes them possible for many climbers. Most are long and complex, especially when the approach and descent are considered to make only one bottom-to-top foray per day possible for most parties.

Of all the Leavenworth areas described, Snow Creek Wall has the most wilderness feel, often a welcome change from the pressures of the other areas.

Snow Creek Wall is one of the most massive faces of rock found in this guide. Approximately a quarter-mile wide, it varies in height from several hundred feet to around 750 feet in the Shield area. Easily viewed head-on from the Snow Lakes Trail, most of the major features can be discerned, which should allow parties to locate their chosen routes.

The most striking feature of the wall on first view is perhaps the massive Shield, lying just left of center. Bounded on the left by the Galaxy dihedral and on the right by the Northern Dihedral, the Shield is the site of Outer Space and many of the other longer routes. Three-fourths of the way up, left of Galaxy, is a long horizontal roof. A number of routes, including Orbit, skirt this roof on its left edge. Directly below the left boundary is the 250-foot Mary Jane Dihedral. At the base of Mary Jane, a 45-degree roof slants off to the left. Orbit travels under this roof, then turns it on its left side.

Shortly left of Orbit, the wall begins to curve around and eventually changes into dirty, broken ground. Just before the wall ends, the first two pitches of Satellite are visible from the Snow Lakes Trail; Satellite's other pitches blend into the face and cannot be seen from the trail. The starts of Orbit to Satellite may take some exploration on the part of those unfamiliar with the area. A third-class "trail" starts left of the Galaxy slab and provides access to these routes. Satellite and Chton are best observed from the descent trail.

To the right of the Shield, the striking White Slab is obvious. Country Club Ramp is the broken ramp above the Slab; Grand Arch forms the right side of a large, smooth face and lies above the start of Country Club Ramp. King Kong and Tempest are the large chimney systems accessible from partway up the ramp. Easter Tower's summit is some 350 feet above the trail's base, and the Champagne route above. April Fool's Tower lies at a similar height near the extreme north (right) side of the wall. A good trail provides access to all these routes.

Descend climbs from Tempest to Satellite by walking and scrambling along the left (south) margin of the wall. Near the bottom, a number of variations lead back to the main trail. The easiest stays as high as possible, uses one short rappel, and then follows the Orbit trail. If one is unfamiliar with the descent and is caught by darkness, it is best to bivouac. Even many of those familiar with the trail don't plan on trying to descend if it gets too late. They plan, instead, on the safer alternative of building a fire and waiting till morning.

The Grand Arch to Nailway routes involve double-rope rappels. Champagne and Spring Fever use the north trail. Those wishing to do Chicken on a Leash and are unfamiliar with the trail, are advised to locate it from Champagne, for the trail can be difficult to locate from below. The north trail descent requires one 75-foot rappel and an interesting exit before the trail is located. Various routes on April Fool's Tower are approached from below via this trail.

LEFT SIDE

A. SATELLITE
II, 5.7; nuts to 1″

Near the end of the wall is a large, right-facing corner. Climb easy cracks left of this corner to a fir tree. Continue 100 ft. to a small tree. Move right over a small roof to a belay above a horizontal crack. A long pitch follows, belaying above a section of white rock. After a short pitch through a roof, a long moderate pitch leads to a ledge. Several options to the top are available.

B. CHTON (TONG)
III, 5.9 +; nuts to 2″

The first pitch belays in a hole near the left edge of a long semi-rotten roof. About 110 ft. higher is a belay ledge. Next take a crack to a hanging belay under a small roof. Another pitch leads to a belay under a slightly larger roof. Move left of this roof and up under the route's largest roof. Pass through this final obstacle onto easier ground. The Lost Planet Airmen variation climbs under the lowest roof to join Chton for three pitches. One pitch moves right to join Orbit at the large ledge. After the knob pitch, move right and finish near the top of Galaxy and Waltz.

C. ORBIT
III, 5.8; nuts to 3″

After a pitch to the base of the Mary Jane Dihedral, move left on a ramp to clean cracks which end at a large block. Move right to a hanging belay under a shallow, left-facing corner. The corner leads to knobs, a large ledge, then huge knobs to the top. Variation, 5.10: from the block, move left over roofs, then back right.

D. MARY JANE DIHEDRAL
III, 5.9; nuts to 2″

The prominent dihedral joins Orbit at the top of the shallow corner. Variation, 5.10a.

E. CHIMNEY SWEEP
III, 5.10b; nuts to 2″

Angle right on ledges below the Mary Jane Dihedral to a chimney close to the Galaxy tree. Climb up and left to join Orbit at the top of the shallow corner.

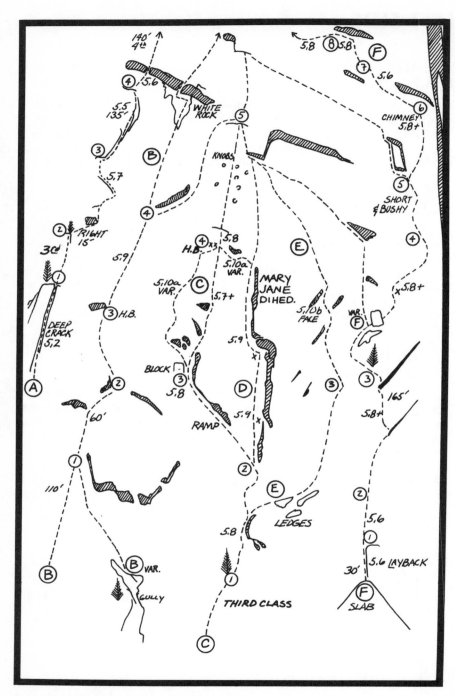

SNOW CREEK WALL: LEFT SIDE

F. GALAXY
III, 5.8+; nuts to 3"

The route begins at the top of a small white slab some 300 ft. below a large fir tree. Two pitches move into the huge, left-facing dihedral. Three more pitches containing chimneys, cracks and faces belay below a roof shortly below the top. One more difficult move leads to easy ground. Variation: two pitches above the tree, angle left to join Orbit above the knob pitch.

G. WALTZ
III, 5.8+

Follow Galaxy to the block above the Galaxy tree. Move out left under a roof, then climb left to shortly above the Orbit-Chimney Sweep junction. Up and right, just left of the long roof, cross the ledge system used by the Galaxy variation. Finally, move up to a shallow right-angling roof and join Galaxy to the top. There are four pitches in total.

THE SHIELD

H. ICONOCLAST
III, 5.10c; nuts to 3"

Climb Remorse or R.P.M.-Remorse to the huge ledge with a tree on its left edge. Face climb left past a bolt to a crack and a belay. The second pitch passes roofs to a blocky ledge. A long, strenuous pitch leads up a corner to end at some small trees. Traverse right 40 ft., follow chickenheads to a crack, then move on to Outer Space. Variation: at the small trees, move left to join Galaxy.

I. R.P.M.
III, 5.10d; nuts to 2"

A difficult pitch up a white slab is followed by crossing Remorse, climbing a right-facing corner and roof, then belaying on Two-Tree Ledge. Twenty feet right of Outer Space is a short system ending at the bush at the beginning of the Outer Space traverse. Next, move left past a bolt onto a dike, then up a shallow dihedral to a mantle. Move right at a bolt to a belay, then join Outer Space to the top of the Pedestal. Rather unprotected climbing leads straight above the Pedestal for two pitches; try long, ½-in. runners for tying off knobs.

J. REMORSE
III, 5.8; nuts to 3″

Scrambling leads to a belay on a dirt ledge, 100 ft. above the ground and 150 ft. below Two-Tree Ledge. The first pitch is mainly a traverse left to the large ledge below and left of Two Tree. The next pitch leads to Two Tree via one of two variations. From near the right end of the ledge, climb to the belay at the finish of the Outer Space traverse. Follow Outer Space to the top of the Pedestal. Two clean pitches angle up and right towards the Country Club Ramp. The standard route joins the ramp. Variation: from the last belay, go straight up past a bolt.

K. OUTER SPACE
III, 5.8 +; nuts to 3″

Two pitches lead up broken ground to the right edge of Two-Tree Ledge. A more difficult start goes up a corner directly beneath the right edge of the ledge. From the ledge's left margin, climb a crack, then follow the traverse right to a bush. The next pitch angles left, then up to the Pedestal. Two 150-ft. pitches lead up the crack to several moderate variations.

L. NORTHERN DIHEDRAL
III, 5.9; nuts to 2″

Pass Two-Tree Ledge on the right, then belay some 60 ft. higher. The first pitch ends under a roof. Climb a wide crack to a corner and follow the corner to a large ledge. Another long pitch leads to the Country Club Ramp.

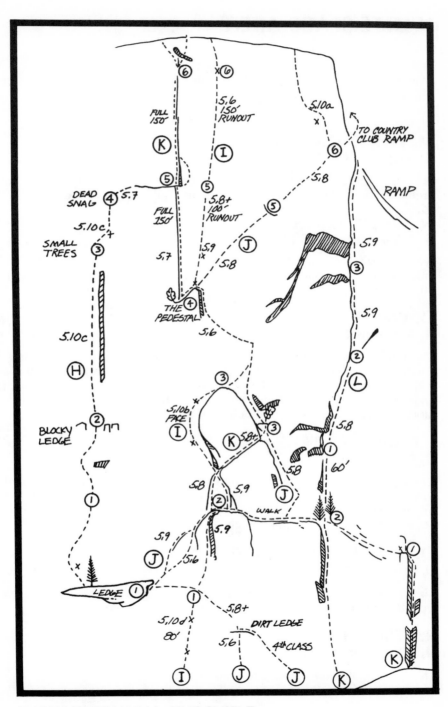

SNOW CREEK WALL: THE SHIELD

WHITE SLABS AREA

In this area, the easy (5.4) Country Club Ramp is valuable for approaches.

M. WHITE SLABS DIRECT
II, 5.9; nuts to 2½"

Start up the Outer Space scramble to a belay. Several pitches, left of the prominent water streaks, lead to the Country Club Ramp.

N. WHITE FRIGHT
II, 5.9 +; nuts to 2"

A large corner is on the left side of the Umbrella Tree face. Left of this, a 90-ft. crack, starting off some flakes, leads to a belay from a horn. More cracks lead up.

O. WHITE SLABS
II, 5.7; nuts to 2"

One hundred feet above the ground, right of the water streaks, is a large tree. Fourth class leads to this tree, where a long pitch leads to a belay just right of a white dihedral. Enter the dihedral, then belay at a bush. One more short pitch ends on the Country Club Ramp. Finish by continuing up the messy ramp or rappelling back down the ramp's other side.

P. UMBRELLA TREE
II, 5.7; nuts to 1"

Climb past the large tree on the Country Club Ramp to where the route begins to traverse left. The Umbrella Tree is visible above. Face climb for two pitches; pass the Tree to a chimney system which is followed for 2½ pitches. Some parties prefer to rappel from the Umbrella Tree.

Q. KING KONG CHIMNEY
II, 5.8; nuts to 2½"

This is the left-hand of two chimney systems just above the large tree on Country Club Ramp. Some loose blocks may be encountered.

R. TEMPEST
II, 5.9 +; nuts to 2"

This is the right-hand chimney referred to in the King Kong route.

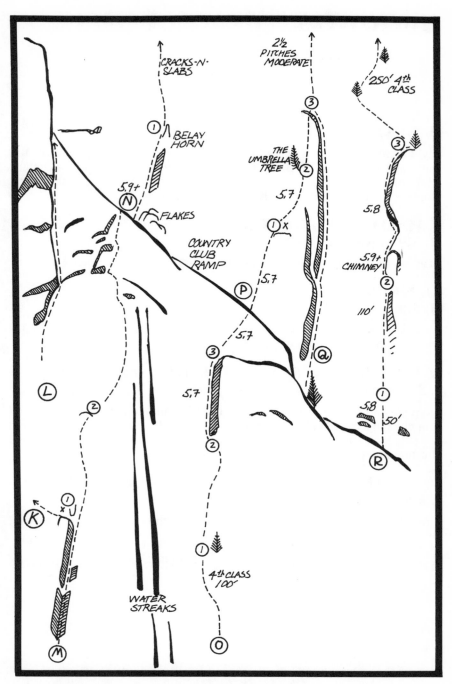

SNOW CREEK WALL: WHITE SLABS AREA

THE TOWERS

S. GRAND ARCH
II, 5.10c; nuts to 2"

Right and above the start of the Country Club Ramp is a single pine. From this pine, angle left for a full pitch, gaining only some 50 ft. of vertical height. Move up via face holds to the arch; follow the arch to a belay at a small tree. Another pitch leads up the arch to the top. Rappel to descend.

T. HALLOWEEN BUTTRESS
II, 5.9 +, A0; nuts to 2"

Start near Grand Arch and do several pitches of largely unknown climbing.

U. NAILWAY
II, 5.9

Nailway is the obvious, left-facing corner left of Champagne. The rating is mostly rumor and is probably much too low. Rappel the route.

V. EASTER TOWER, NOTCH ROUTE (not shown)
I, 5.7; nuts to 1"

From the trail near the cliff's base, 300 ft. of scrambling with some fourth and fifth class in a major gully system lead to a notch between the main wall and the detached Easter Tower. Obvious cracks lead up from the notch, where a short rappel leads back down.

W. EASTER TOWER, THE NORTH FACE (not shown)
I, 5.8; nuts to 2"

Drop down under the north face and climb slightly rotten cracks past old, fixed pins to the top.

X. EASTER TOWER, THE OUTSIDE FACE (not shown)

This involves three aid pitches.

Y. CHAMPAGNE
II, 5.7; nuts to 2½"

From the Easter Tower notch, climb flakes to a ledge, traverse left, then move up through a break in a long, horizontal roof. From the belay, traverse right 30 ft. to a major, right-facing corner. From the grassy ledge at the corner's top, take a black and white chimney to the top. Scramble right to locate a rappel, then follow the north descent trail.

Z. SPRING FEVER
II, 5.8; nuts to 2"

About 40 ft. north of the Easter Tower notch, climb up to the right edge of the same ledge Champagne uses. Step right past a bolt, then face climb up to the corner mentioned in Champagne. From a belay, move out right of the corner to the grassy ledge. From the ledge's right side, a short crack, a traverse leads into the woods.

AA. CHICKEN ON A LEASH
I, 5.10b; nuts to 2"

Near the end of Spring Fever, a striking white corner-crack leads one pitch to the cliff's top. Rappel back down to the base.

BB. VICIOUS RUMOR (not shown)
I, 5.11a; nuts to 2"

Near the base of April Fool's Tower, this route is a 45-ft., 110-degree crack.

CC. RIVER GUANGE (not shown)
I, 5.6

Climb the cracks and knobs seen from Vicious Rumor.

DD. GUIARDIA BUTTRESS (not shown)
I, 5.8

These two pitches may be seen from the Icicle Road.

EE. APRIL FOOL'S TOWER, THE NOTCH ROUTE (not shown)
I, 5.8; nuts to 2"

A short rappel leads back down.

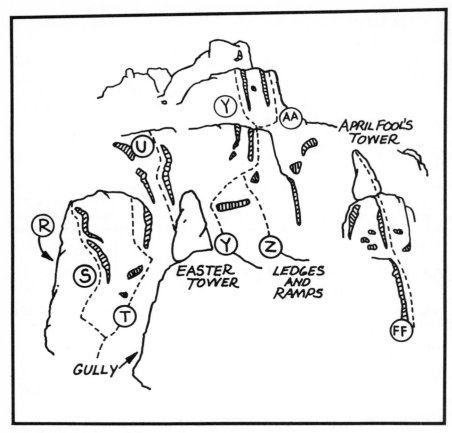

SNOW CREEK WALL: THE TOWERS

FF. APRIL FOOL'S TOWER, TARKUS
II, 5.9; nuts to 3″

This is a climb on the outside face of the tower.

GG. APRIL FOOL'S TOWER, OVERHANG CORNER (not shown)
I, 5.9 +; nuts to 4″

This is a route near the notch.

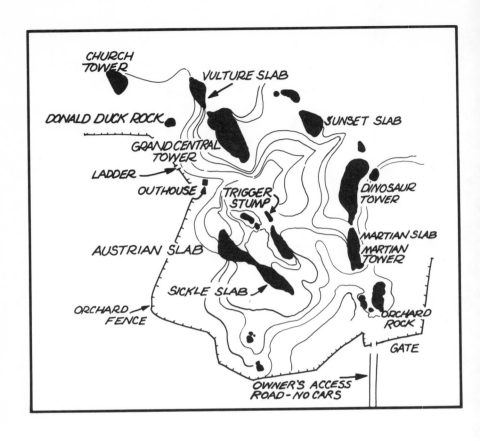

PESHASTIN PINNACLES

The Peshastin Pinnacles are unique in Washington climbing in that they make up the only major area where the rock is neither granitic nor volcanic. The rock, complete with its own character and problems, is a rather soft Swauk Sandstone. The character, once experienced, is self explanatory; the problems are less so.

The problems, generally, are twofold: overpopulation and fragile rock. The number of people on a May weekend can stifle the person who wished to climb in private. The fragile rock can pose more serious problems. Piton damage is severe on the routes that once allowed their placement. Furthermore, the indiscriminate use of bolts, some poorly placed on established routes, mars the climbs' beauty. More serious is the potential for pebbles and flakes to suddenly explode. This can be a critical problem if you're at the top of The West Face Direct and a pebble pops; an 80-foot ground fall could result. Another difficulty is rating climbs when their features change. Cajun Queen on Austrian Slab is a prime example of this phenomenon. At various times in its climbing history, its ratings have fluctuated between 5.8 and 5.10. Another, more dramatic example is that of Trigger Finger. Once one of the more spectacular spires of the Northwest, it fell over in January of 1978, leaving only a stump. On 95 percent of the Peshastin routes, this problem is negligible. The climbs are in much the same state as when they were first climbed; but it is always best to keep these cautions in mind.

With these deterrents one may well ask, "why climb at the 'Clees'?" (as the Pinnacles were referred to in the mid-seventies). The reasons are numerous and include the friendly, unintimidating nature of the area, the best weather and earliest rock-climbing season in Washington and the delightful nature of the climbs themselves.

The Pinnacles are visible from U.S. 2 between the towns of Leavenworth and Cashmere. A paved road through the orchards heads north off the main highway to the dirt access road immediately below the lowest crags. The parking situation is currently in a state of flux so follow directions on the posted signs. Failure to do so will result in your car being ticketed or towed away.

Both the Pinnacles and the surrounding orchards are owned by the same people. The area is closed during fruit-picking time, usually early September through mid-October, due in part to climber-initiated problems. Please cross fences only through gates; don't block access roads or abuse the property in any manner. Again, the Pinnacles are privately owned, so all climbers must respect the owners' wishes in order to keep this unique area open.

Today it may not be as necessary as before to stress the need to keep pitons out of this fragile area. As early as 1960, Fred Beckey wrote, "Climbers who regularly practice climb in the Peshastin Pinnacles report an influx of bolt placing on already established routes. Routes generally have been done with sufficient bolts for protection and the nailing of extra iron serves only to ruin the routes for others."[4] All climbs are either bolt protected or safely protected with nuts.

Soon, a concerted effort to rebuild the trail must take place in order to slow the tremendous erosion of the past years. In the meantime, please stay on the established trails. Outhouse facilities are located at the base of Grand Central Tower.

---

[4]Fred Beckey, "Too Much Iron," *The Mountaineer*, Vol. 53, No. 4, (1960), p. 94.

ORCHARD ROCK

Orchard Rock is the first small feature one comes to when entering the Pinnacles. The routes' names tend to be fairly descriptive of the problems involved. Descent is by a 75-foot rappel or by down climbing the Scramble.

A. THE RIDGE (not shown)
I, 5.0

Start at the toe and climb semi-rotten rock.

B. THE SCRAMBLE
I, 5.0; runners for protection

On the west face, climb up to a large diagonally running ramp to a notch. A more difficult variation is to start near the toe of the rock and climb to the notch. A short second pitch, passing by the Womb, leads to the top.

C. C. CRACK
I, 5.10a

This is the wide crack right of the notch.

D. THE OVERHANG
I, 5.8 +

This climb on the west face has minimal fixed protection.

E. THE TUNNEL
I, 5.6; nuts to 2"

This route starts from the upper side of the rock.

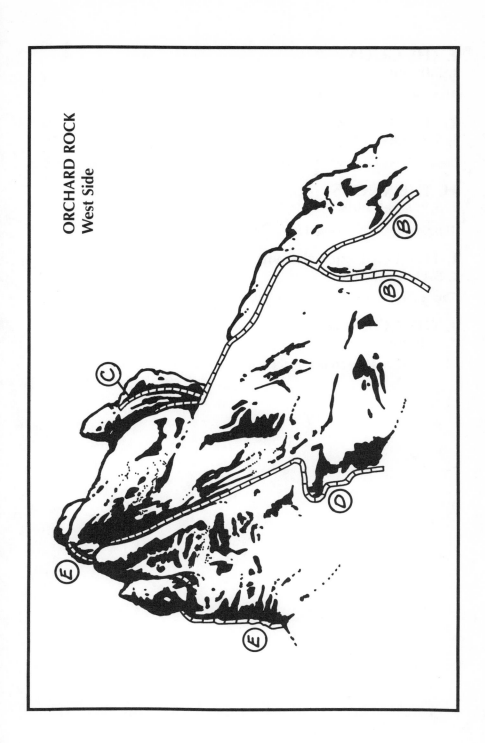

ORCHARD ROCK
West Side

F. THE GULLY
I, 5.0; nuts to 1″

This climb is on the east face.

G. THE CRACK
I, 5.7; nuts to 1½″

Start in The Gully, then step left.

H. THE KNOBS
I, 5.9; small nuts

The Knobs is just downhill from The Gully.

I. THE TUBE (not shown)
I, 5.11; small nuts

This is the thin slot left of The Knobs.

J. THE CORNER
I, 5.0; nuts to 1″

This is a short little corner on the east face that joins The Scramble.

ORCHARD ROCK
East Side

MARTIAN TOWER

The little summit just uphill from Orchard Rock is Martian Tower. From its summit one can do a 75-foot rappel down the "back side" or continue on The Ridge Route.

A. THE RIDGE ROUTE
I, 5.6; nuts to 1"

From the Tower's east side, climb to the notch, then continue along the ridge crest. The climb takes three pitches. The notch can also be approached from the slab side.

B. CATACOMBS
I, 5.8; fixed protection and runners

Follow an obvious line leading through a series of wind caves. A 5.7 corner lies off to the right.

C. GRAHAM CRACKERS
I, 5.10b; fixed protection

Climb past two bolts to join either Catacombs or Butter Brickle.

D. BUTTER BRICKLE
I, 5.9; nuts to 2"

From a notch at the toe of the rock, move out left to follow a short crack into the Bathtub formations.

E. FROSTBACK FOLLIES
I, 5.10a; nuts to 2"

These are the roofs left of the Brickle.

F. THE WEST FACE
I, 5.8; nuts to 1″

Climb up the slab until it's possible to move right onto the Tower.

G. SPIRAL
I, 5.6; nuts to 2″

Follow The West Face to the belay below the Tower. Next, climb into the notch, then spiral around the Tower's west face to the summit.

MARTIAN TOWER

MARTIAN SLAB

This long slab, badly eroded at its base, leads from Martian Tower up to near the start of Dinosaur Tower. The routes all lie on the west face. Most climbs work up to the uphill side where a short, 5.7 down climb or rappel leads off.

A. THE RIDGE ROUTE (see previous page)

B. MARTIAN DIAGONAL
I, 5.6; nuts to 1″

Starting somewhere near the lower edge of the slab, numerous variations funnel to a belay just below a prominent ramp. Another pitch and a half continue along this ramp.

C. MARTIAN DIRECT
I, 5.8; fixed protection

From the first Martian Diagonal belay, the left of two distinctive lines of pockets leads to The Ridge Route.

D. DIAGONAL BYPASS
I, 5.5; fixed protection

Climb Martian Diagonal to the first belay, then move left, then up to rejoin the ramp.

E. SERPENT
I, 5.7; fixed protection

A diagonally leading line of pockets. From the start (on the ground) of these pockets, go straight up past several bolts, then over a small roof to a belay on the ramp. A 165-ft. rope is needed.

F. VOYAGER ONE
I, 5.6; fixed protection

Farther up the hill from Serpent, a small cave lies a short distance above the ground. Follow a line of bolts right of this cave to the ramp. A 165-ft. rope is needed.

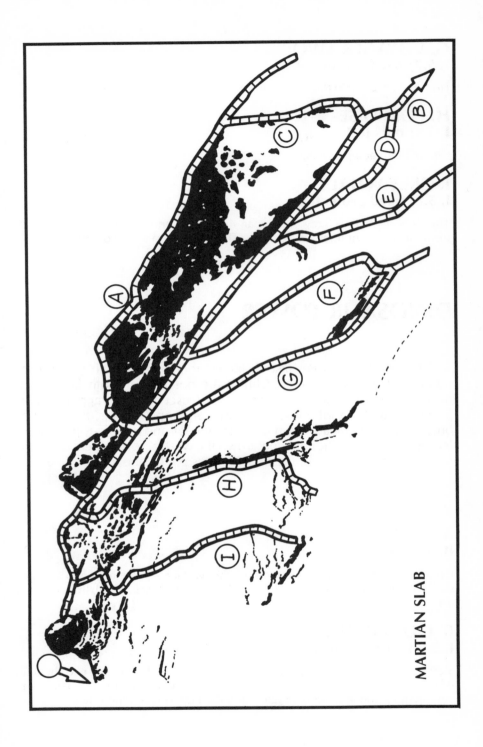

MARTIAN SLAB

G. VOYAGER TWO
I, 5.7; fixed protection

From the cave move left and up to the ramp. A 165-ft. rope is needed.

H. PORPOISE
I, 5.4; nuts to 1"

Climb a left-facing corner.

I. GREY WHALE
I, 5.8; fixed protection

This is the obvious grey slab near the uphill end of Martian Slab. Two distinctly different lines are possible. The left one uses only one bolt.

DINOSAUR TOWER

Dinosaur Tower is Peshastin's largest rock and as such contains a number of excellent routes. Climbs are possible on both faces, but most of the routes lie on the west side. Descent is via rappel from a point below the northern summit. Two one-rope rappels, the second only 10 feet long, lead down the east face, or one double-rope rappel leaves the same anchor but goes down the west face. Another common rappel is from the end of the first Potholes pitch; one rope suffices.

A. SKYLINE
II, 5.5; nuts to 2"

From the highest point of ground under the west face, scramble up to a ledge which leads right to a deep crack on the left side of a block. Climb this crack to a small tree, then continue for several more pitches.

B. OUT OF REACH
I, 5.8 to 5.11; nuts to 1½"

Start up a groove above the left end of the Skyline ledge. Traverse to the left edge of the huge roof to make the reach, the difficulty of which depends on your height. Above the roof, angle right, then up to reach the ridge.

C. POTHOLES
I, 5.7 +; fixed protection

Start near the previous routes and angle up and left on obvious holds, 5.6, to a semi-hanging belay. The second pitch goes up to a notch, then over the other side to the belay/rappel.

D. POTHOLES DIRECT
I, 5.10b; fixed protection

Step over a small roof under the first Potholes belay.

E. POTHOLES DIRECT DIRECT
I, 5.10a; fixed protection

This is the shallow, left-facing corner under the Potholes belay.

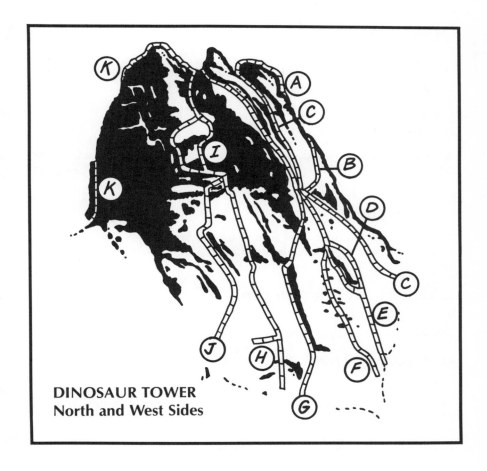

DINOSAUR TOWER
North and West Sides

F. WASHBOARDS
I, 5.10c; fixed protection

Obvious climbing leads to the Potholes belay. A variation from the top of the Boards joins Primate.

G. PRIMATE
I, 5.10d; fixed protection

Start up an easy, white flake or a 5.9 face to the right of the flake to a semi-hanging belay. The second pitch follows an old bolt line to the Potholes belay.

H. DR. LEAKEY
I, 5.10b; fixed protection

Ever steepening rock left of the Primate flake leads to a large ledge beneath a roof. A direct start is 5.11.

I. CRO MAGNON
I, 5.8; nuts to 2"

From the ledge mentioned on Leakey, climb a crack up and right, then up to the top.

J. CAVEMAN
I, 5.9 +; nuts to 2"

Angle up to a corner left of Leakey, then continue up to the accommodating ledge. From the left end of the ledge, pass bolts up and around to the rappel.

K. PILTDOWN
I, 5.7; nuts to 1½"

From the north notch, boulder a move up to a large ledge. Continue straight above the ledge's right side. The variation is 5.8 and starts a few feet west of the notch.

L. SHORT BITE (not shown)
I, 5.8 +

This short crack climb is located on a boulder that helps to form the notch.

M. MISSING LINK
I, 5.8

This poor route is started down the east side of the notch. Follow ramps up, then climb the flaky trough of the rappel route.

N. MICKEY MOUSE CRACK
I, 5.8; nuts to 3″

This is a short crack that requires a fair amount of poor climbing to reach it. Join Skyline.

O. HOLE IN THE WALL
I, 5.5

Traverse out left on a ledge to the middle section of Mickey Mouse. Below the final crack, traverse left, then pass through a tunnel to the west side of the Tower.

DINOSAUR TOWER
East Side

SUNSET SLAB

Sunset Slab routes are some of the friendliest at Peshastin, especially in the Sunset to National Velvet area. The generous supply of holds seems to make route descriptions meaningless as one can go almost anywhere one pleases. Descents are also simple, involving either single-rope, low-angle rappels or an easy walk off through a tunnel.

A. CONTINUOUS B.S.
I, 5.6 or 5.9; minimal fixed protection

Various starts somewhere around several small pines or at a bush farther uphill lead past a bolt to a belay in a ledge/corner. Staying left past the bolt increases the difficulty; moving right decreases it. One more pitch leads up a rib left of a little trough to the unroping point.

B. GREEN VELVET
I, 5.8; minimal protection with small nuts and bolts

Starting near a large tree, climb up to several tiny caves, up past a bolt, then left to a belay in a large corner. Continue up easy rock or rappel back down.

C. NATIONAL VELVET
I, 5.6; fixed protection

A line of bolts leads up to the Green Velvet belay.

D. BOOBY VINTON
I, 5.5; fixed protection

A line of bolts leads to a pine tree 75 ft. above the ground and just left of the corner. The bolts on this route and National Velvet can be combined in almost any fashion.

E. 5.5 ROUTE
I, 5.5; fixed protection

Three bolts protect a line right of the Sunset crack.

F. SUNSET
I, 5.4; fixed protection

A little crack or groove leads to the pine tree mentioned in Booby Vinton. From the tree, it is possible to traverse left to join Sunrise at the crack.

G. SUNRISE
I, 5.7; nuts to 2″

Uphill from Sunset, climb past two bolts to the belay at the base of an obvious crack. Moderate climbing leads up this somewhat rotten crack to a tree.

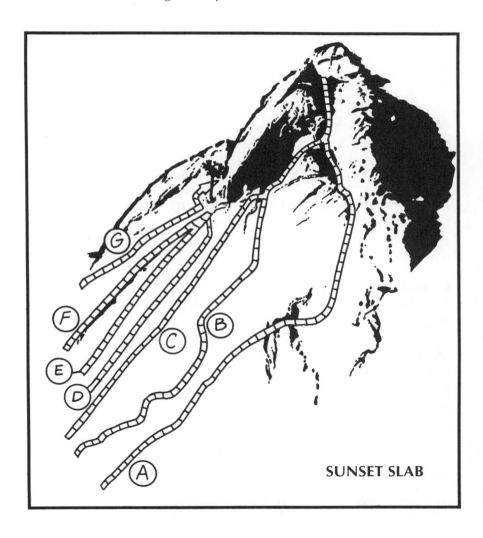

SUNSET SLAB

GRAND CENTRAL TOWER

Grand Central Tower is like Dinosaur in that it has climbs on both its east and west faces, each of different character. Those on the sunny, west face tend to be face routes, many of them somewhat decomposed. The east-face routes, on the other hand, are basically steep, crack climbs. Several descents are used. From the end of Empire State or from the top of the second pitch of Lightning, a one-rope, overhanging rappel leads down the east side. From the summit, a single-rope rappel leads down the east face to the upper notch. The third common rappel is from the end of the first pitch of the west-face route. A 150-foot rope comes close enough to the ground to do the job.

A. NIRVANA RIDGE
II, 5.8+; small nuts

The route approximately follows the south ridge, occasionally venturing out onto the west face. Some sections of questionable rock are encountered.

B. SUNSHINE AHEAD (not shown)
I, 5.10a

A crack on the southeast face leads up to Nirvana Ridge. The protection is somewhat poor.

C. BOMB SHELTER
I, 5.11a

Most parties rappel after the first pitch.

D. VERTIGO
I, 5.8; nuts to 3"

Follow the skid marks above the notch. Vertigo Direct, 5.9, takes the wide flake above the start.

E. CORKSCREW
I, 5.9; nuts to 2"

Two feet right of Vertigo, pass two poor bolts until it is possible to traverse right to the chimney that forms the upper section of Empire State. A second pitch, this one on the west face, leads to the top.

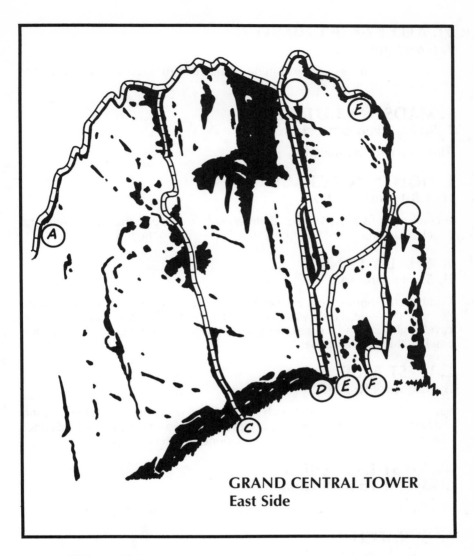

GRAND CENTRAL TOWER
East Side

F. EMPIRE STATE
I, 5.7; nuts to 3″

Traverse under a deep cave to the chimney mentioned in the previous route. A direct start is 5.8 +. The climb ends on a good ledge.

G. FAT MAN'S CHIMNEY (JOCK TRAP)
I, 5.8 +; nuts to 2″

Walk downhill, north, from Empire State to an obvious chimney.

H. ALLEY OOP CHIMNEY
I, 5.8 +; nuts to 2"

Right of Fat Man's is another chimney reached from below or from the end of the first Lightning pitch.

I. MADSEN'S BUTTRESS
I, 5.10a; fixed protection

This is on decomposed rock.

J. LIGHTNING CRACK
II, 5.8 +; nuts to 2½"

A crack pitch right of Madsen's Buttress leads to a ledge beneath the Lightning Crack. From the top of Lightning, join Corkscrew to the top.

K. SHADY LANE
II, 5.8 +; nuts to 3"

Climb a crack/groove to a cave right of the Lightning route's first ledge. From the cave's left side, it is easy to traverse to Lightning. The Shady Lane leaves the cave's right side and passes three bolts on decomposed rock to climb a wide crack to the summit rappel.

L. WEST FACE
II, 5.8; nuts to 2½"

Most parties only do the first pitch, which is the area's best protected after the first bolt is reached. The second pitch proceeds up a chimney. The third either joins Corkscrew or the wide crack mentioned in Shady Lane.

M. WEST FACE DIRECT
I, 5.10a; fixed protection

This line runs directly into the West Face cave with minimal protection.

N. SCRATCH
I, 5.10b; fixed protection

Scratch lies right of West Face Direct, ends in the same cave and features the same type of protection.

O. SANDBOX
II, 5.9; nuts to 2½"

Rotten rock—that says it all.

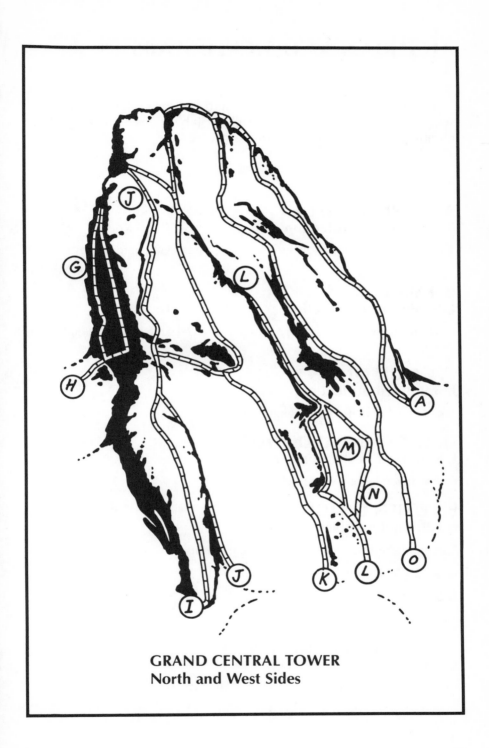

GRAND CENTRAL TOWER
North and West Sides

AUSTRIAN AND SICKLE SLABS

It is best to scramble off Austrian Slab after one pitch, for the upper section is quite decomposed. Sickle Slab is descended by down climbing off the north end of the ridge.

A. SLENDER THREAD
I, 5.9 +; fixed protection

This route follows a shallow groove above a tree being uprooted by climber-initiated erosion.

B. FAKIN' IT
I, 5.9 +; fixed protection

From the low point of the slab, pass a bolt, then take the left line of bolts to the ledge.

C. CAJUN QUEEN
I, 5.9; fixed protection

Take the right line from the Fakin' It bolt.

D. THE STANDARD ROUTE
I, 5.8; fixed protection.

Follow several grooves just right of center.

E. LICHEN DELIGHT
I, 5.9; minimal fixed protection

This climbs the face right of The Standard Route.

F. SLAKIN
I, 5.8; fixed protection

Slakin is a short line left of a smooth, white face.

G. THE TREE (not shown)
I, 5.4

Climb terrible rock up a groove left of Windward Direct.

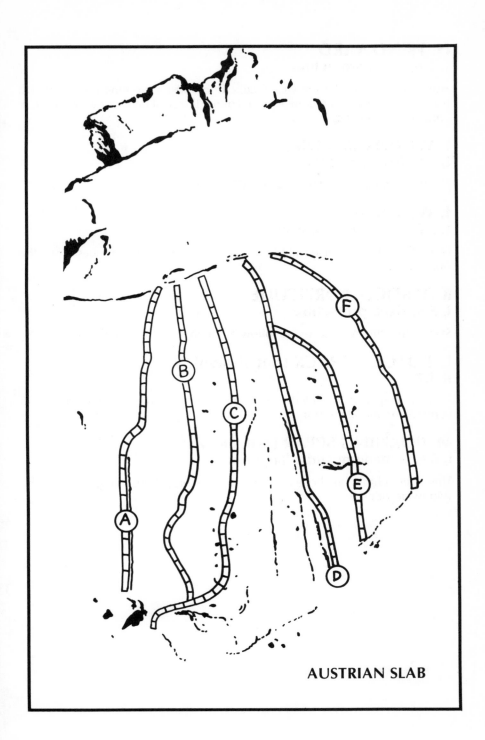

AUSTRIAN SLAB

H. WINDWARD
I, 5.6; fixed protection

From the notch under the west face, climb up to a prominent ledge which leads out and right to the ridge crest. Follow the crest north for another pitch. Variation: A direct start is 5.8.

I. WINDWARD DIRECT
I, 5.8; fixed protection

Continue straight past the ledge on Windward.

J. WINDCAVE
I, 5.8; fixed protection and runners

From the notch, traverse right to a cave. Another pitch continues along the ridge crest.

K. TESTICLE FORTITUDE
I, 5.9; fixed protection

Start below the Windcave and follow a line to its left to join the ridge.

L. ROTGUT CRACK (not shown)
I, 5.7

This is a deep, rotten crack downhill from the Windcave. It is then possible to continue up along the ridge.

M. BURNING SPEAR (not shown)
I, 5.6; a medium and a large nut

This short climb on the east face leads, after a bouldering start, to the Windward ridge belay.

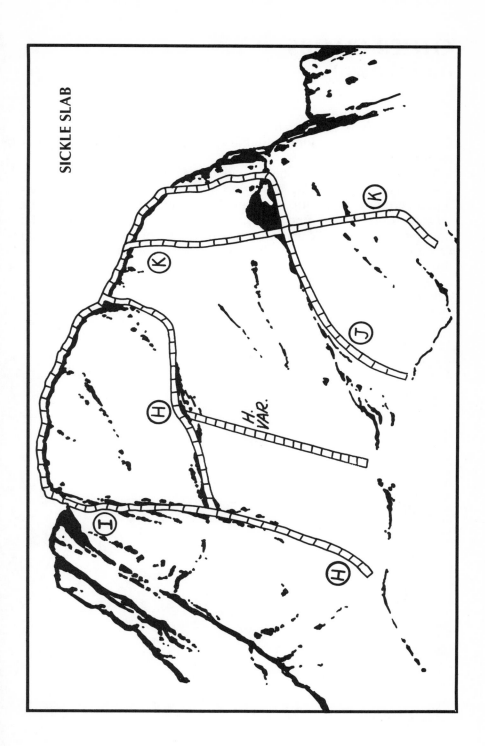

SICKLE SLAB

OTHER CLIMBS
(not shown)

The west face of Church Tower has two 5.7 routes. The rotten Chimney Sweep is the left line; the slightly better right-hand route is called the Steeple route.

Vulture Slab has three rotten routes. The Vulture route, 5.8, leads up a white groove to a belay. A second pitch follows ramps and a low-angle chimney to the top. Condor, 5.8, climbs past bolts left of the Vulture route to the first belay. Buzzard, 5.4, follows horizontal parallel cracks left of Condor to the upper section of that route. Both Condor and Buzzard end at this point. The upper pitch of Vulture is 5.6.

Donald Duck is the small pinnacle with bouldering routes. The remains of the Trigger Finger are easily climbed.

MISCELLANEOUS SANDSTONE CRAGS

East of Leavenworth 2.2 miles on U.S. Highway 2 is Sandy Slab, a piece of rock immediately adjacent to the road. On the left side, 50 feet above the road and next to a group of pines, is Get Your Wings, a 5.8 route. The pitch is fixed, as are all routes on this slab, and ends at a small pine. It is possible to traverse off left or rappel with two ropes. Never on Sunday, 5.7, starts just right of Wings in a flaky depression and ends at the same tree. Down at road level and right of Never on Sunday is A-1, a 5.6 route. The first 80-foot pitch passes two aluminum bolt hangers to a belay at a pocket. The route finishes with a 150-foot pitch up and left to a tree. Another 30 feet farther right, a bolt will be seen some 20 to 30 feet up, above some small roofs. Both I Shot My Baby and Fascist Rule use this first bolt, although it can be reached via one of several lines. Baby takes a leftward line to reach a prominent pine 165 feet up. This 5.8 route passes three bolts before reaching the tree. Two more short pitches finish off the right side. Fascist Rule is also 5.8 and is less protected than Baby. On the extreme right end of Sandy Slab is Suncups, a 5.8 + or 5.9 route. The first pitch ends at a large tree. From the tree, either walk off or continue up an easy but unprotected rib.

Near the town of Peshastin, towards Derby Canyon, is another slab, S. Slab. Park on a dirt road where the paved road veers 90 degrees left. Walk down the railroad tracks to the slab with the fence at its base. Lilies of the Field, a fixed 5.7 route, passes bolts left of two prominent corners to a belay on the iron rods which run across the face. Another pitch continues up and off. Catching the Sun passes a bolt between the two corners to eventually finish at the same place as Lilies. Catching is also a 5.7 route. Be sure to carry at least four runners for each route to tie off iron rods.

Chumstick Snag is a pinnacle located four miles from Leavenworth on the Plain Road. Turn left up Spromberg Canyon and park at its end. Pass through the meadow, then up the ridge dividing it for about a half mile until Chumstick and its neighbor, Stick Snag, are reached. Chumstick's standard route, a 5.7 climb requiring nuts to ¾ inch, starts on the southwest corner of the rock. Traverse down until it is possible to climb up potholes to the summit ridge. A single-rope rappel leads back down. The Southwest Face aid route is usually fixed and requires some 5.8 free climbing as well as some aid.

INDEX